بسم الله الرحمن الرحيم

BUSTĀN AL-ʿĀRIFĪN

GARDEN OF THE AWARE

Compiled by
Imam Al-Nawawī

Translated by
Omer El-Hamdoon

KINGSTON OAK TREE INSTITUTE

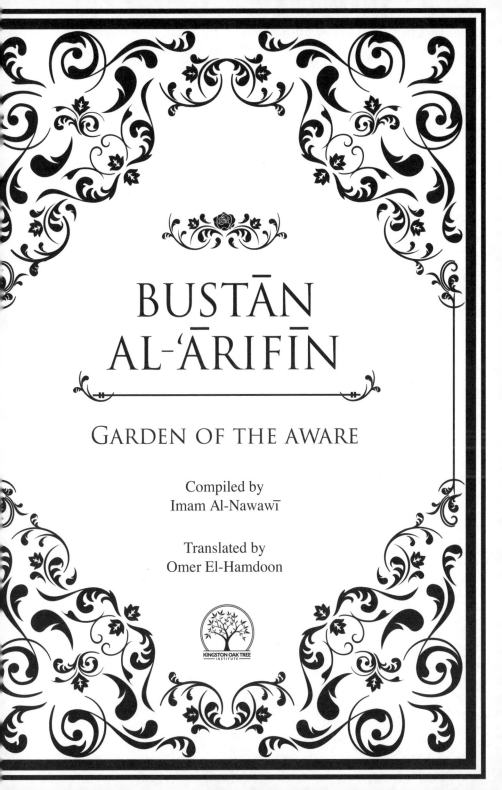

KINGSTON OAK TREE
INSTITUTE

First Published in Great Britain in 2020.

This edition Published in Great Britain in 2020

ISBN: 978-1-9163957-2-5

Designed by:
Hassan Ismaili

Printed by Mega Printing in Turkey

Table of Contents

Transliteration Guide

Alone	Romanization	English words having similar sounds
ا	ā	-
ت	t	true
ث	th	think
ح	ḥ	-
خ	kh	-
ذ	dh	this
ش	sh	show
ص	ṣ	-
ض	ḍ	-
ط	ṭ	-
ظ	ẓ	-
ع	'(ayn)	-
غ	gh	-
ق	q	-
ه ، ة	t or h	-

Vowels and Diphthongs

َ	a	اَ	ā	ىِ	ī
ُ	u	ىَ	ā	َوْ	aw
ِ	i	وُ	ū	َىْ	ay

Translator's Foreword

In October 2019, I began a series of circles in Kingston Masjid. On contemplating the subject to be delivered, I was in favour of studying and delivering on a topic that may not be widely addressed as one would hope, that is the Purification of the Soul.

It was at this junction, that the book Bustān al-'Ārifīn (بستان العارفين) came to mind. Despite it being a short text, it was riddled with useful information and a unique perspective; and written by one of the great medieval Islamic scholars. I didn't hesitate on proceeding with this book. My only concern was to see if there was a translation of this book in English that would simplify my task. I researched and found a work of translation by Aisha Bewley, published by Diwan Press.

I purchased this translation, and hoped to use it as a reference to some difficult words. Whilst the translation was a good attempt and indeed helped me many-a-time, it had a fair share of inaccuracies, which on some occasions totally distorted the meaning. This was coupled with the fact, that the translator omitted – intentionally or not – some words which I thought were necessary. The translator also removed the chains of transmission from the book. Whilst the latter part, I fully understand; I do feel that this renders the work somewhat incomplete. The mention of the chains of transmission, in several places serves a wider application as intended by the author.

Bearing all the above in mind, I began my quest to translate this wonderful book, trying to complement what was missed in Mrs Bewley's translation, and adding to it the parts that were omitted. In addition to this, I favoured a much more literal translation, with much less paraphrasing. This may – on many instances – read strangely: however, I found that closer to the Arabic wordings; and it conveyed pretty much the same concept as it read in the original Arabic.

As I taught the book, I became much more fascinated with the author and his contribution to this book. The core of the book is to affirm the importance of the Next Life and how to prepare for it, through sincerity, truthfulness, knowledge, abstinence, love for the righteous, appreciation of the Help and Aid that Allah gives to His chosen ones in the form of gifts. As I read more into the book, and reflected on the life of the author, it became quite clear to me that a lot of what who he is, comes to light in this book. One example of this was for a long time, I was aware that Imam al-Nawawī lived such a short life, dying at the young age of 45. Yet, when we examine his compilations and contributions to knowledge and academia, we find that his work is extraordinary, exceeding his material lifespan. In this book, you will note how he refers to three scholars who were renowned for this: al-Shāfi'ī, al-'Ash'arī and al-Ghazālī; little being aware that his name is also to be among those high achievers.

Indeed, Imam al-Nawawī is a great inspiration to those who dedicate their lives to the world of knowledge and teaching. Furthermore, he is an example to the rest of us who are still wasting our lives in trivial pursuits. May Allah have mercy on him and raise his status.

As I came to the end of the translation, and as I wrote the last few lines, I felt a kind of emptiness, which I hadn't experienced before. It felt very much that I was bidding farewell to my personal teacher and mentor. I felt a connection with Shaykh ul-Islam which is beyond words.

May Allah have mercy on this great man, which I personally remember him in my *du'ā'*.

Some Points to Consider

The original text of the author has mentioned in some instances his chains of transmission. I have translated these chains, as I felt that this is part of the translation trust. However, I have coloured them in grey, so that the reader can skip through these should he wish.

Some common words or Islamic words that have become part of the English lexicon, then I have chosen not to transliterate it, like the words "Abu" and "Muhammad" or the word "shari'a".

Words which are not English, I have put in italics to help the reader, and in the main you will find these in the Glossary at the end of the book. I have chosen to include the Arabic text for the Quranic verses, and the Prophetic hadith I have put in bold.

You will find these small icons (ﷺ) and (ؓ) which are "*ṣalla Allahu 'alayhi wa sallam*" and "*raḍia Allahu 'anhu*"; and they mean "May Allah send His prayers[1] and greetings on him" and "May Allah be pleased with him" respectively.

1 The prayers of Allah on His creation is His connection to them with His Mercy towards them

The translation of any Arabic text to English reveals the richness and - thence - superiority of the Arabic language. For that reason, it will always remain difficult to translate accurately and precisely. Even as early on in translating the title of the book, it took some effort to find the best translation of "al-'Ārifīn". For this word is much more than simply someone who knows or understands. I chose the word "aware" reluctantly as that was the best word I could find. And the same applies to many other words within the text. I ask Allah to pardon my shortcomings.

Expression of Gratitude

I wish to mention a special thanks to Hassan Ismaili who has once again assisted me in bringing this book out, through his outstanding contribution to the artwork and design of this book. And a further thanks to Dr Eymen Kaya who revised the translation for me, providing valuable suggestions for a better read. *Jazakum Allahu khayra*.

Lastly, I praise Allah the Almighty for allowing me to complete such an endeavour, hoping that this translation adds a drop or two to the ocean of knowledge; for without His aid and support, nothing is possible.

My purest and sincere salutations and greetings to our Prophet Muhammad, who is our foremost teacher, and without him we would have not be guided by Allah to the Straight Path.

"My Lord! Accept from Me, for You are the Most Hearing, Most Knowing!"

Biography of Imam al-Nawawī (631 – 676AH)

Imam al-Nawawī: He is Muḥyi Uddin – Abu Zakariyyā Yaḥyā ibn Sharaf al-Ḥawrānī al-Nawawī al-Shāfi'ī. He is famous as Imam al-Nawawī because of his attribution to his hometown: Nawā. Al-Nawawī was a Sunni jurist of the Shāfi'ī school, as well as being a hadith scholar and appropriately titled as Shaykh al-Islam.

He lived a short life of 45 years but during this short period, he had compiled a large number of books on different subjects and all his books have been recognised as valuable contributions to the Islamic knowledge. More so, some of his compilations are household names which are found extensively in Muslim homes like the Forty Hadith Nawawī, Riyāḍ al-Ṣāliḥīn and the Book of Adhkār.

His Birth and Family

Imam al-Nawawī was born in Muḥarram 631 AH (1233 AD) in the village of Nawā, which is one of the villages of the Ḥawrān region, near the City of Damascus - present day Syria. He did not come from a well-known family. There is very little mention of his father and other relatives. This implies that they were a modest family. They also were not known for producing great scholars. However, his father did have a reputation for being virtuous and pious.

His Childhood

From his youth, Yaḥyā al-Nawawī was not attracted to playing or amusement. Indeed, the other children harassed him for this. From an early age, he turned his attention to his studies. He hated any activity that would take him away from memorising the Quran. On one occasion, the children forced him to play with them and he cried because of the time that he was wasting. It is not surprising then, that he memorised the Quran at an early age, before reaching puberty.

Shaykh Yāsīn al-Marākashī had observed the devotion of young Yaḥyā to learning and his reluctance from playing with other children. He said, "On observing his sagacity and profundity, a special love and affection developed in my heart for young Nawawī. I approached his teacher and urged him to take exceptional care of this lad as he was to become a great religious scholar and most pious saint of future."

The teacher asked, "Are you a soothsayer or an astrologer?"

Yāsīn said, "I am neither a soothsayer nor an astrologer; but Allah caused me to utter these words!"

The teacher conveyed this incident to al-Nawawī's father; and from then on, his father assisted his son in the quest for knowledge. Initially, the young al-Nawawī wanted to study medicine. He purchased the book al-Qānūn[2]. He said that he felt his heart darken. So, he abandoned this and went for Islamic studies.

He decided to dedicate his life for the service and promotion of the cause of Islam and Islamic sciences; and he was aided and supported by his father.

His Pursuit of Knowledge

Imam al-Nawawī lived in his birth town till the age of 18 years. In the year 649 AH, his father took him to Damascus which – at that time – was considered the centre of learning as it housed more than three hundred educational institutes.

He first began his education at the Sāramiyyah school in Damascus. This is where his father had left him. He had no housing there whatsoever. After some time, he approached the head of the school to ask if he had any housing, as many of the schools house their students. They had no housing; and it was suggested that he go to Rawāḥiyyah School.

At this stage, he left the Sāramiyyah school, and went on hajj with his father in 650. On coming back, he enrolled with the Madrasah Rawāḥiyyah. There, he was given a very small room in which he lived for a number of years. It was stated that when one visited him, the room was so small and the books were so many, that the only way one could sit down was to remove the books and pile them on top of each other to make some room.

When he first joined this school, he memorised al-Tanbīh[3] in four

2 Known in English as The Canon of Medicine is an encyclopaedia of medicine in five books compiled by Persian Muslim physician-philosopher Ibn Sīnā (Avicenna) and completed in 1025CE

3 This is a famous fiqh book of Imam al-Shīrāzi (d. 476AH), which is considered an important reference in the Shāfi'ī school

and a half months; and he read the book al-Muhadh-dhab[4] – from memory – in the remainder of that year to his teacher.
He has been reported to have about 12 lessons every day in a variety of sciences including *fiqh* (jurisprudence), hadith, hadith terminology and Arabic. He studied with many great Islamic scholars which he makes mention of some of them in this book between your hands.

During this time, he lived a hard life, eating what bread was offered and sleeping rough.

He remained in that small room at the Rawāḥiyyah, until he was appointed the head of Dar al-Hadith Ashrafiyyah school, a number of years later. He assumed his role as the head in succession to Shaykh Abu Shāmah who had just died. This was at the age of 24. He remained there as the head for eleven years, never accepting any compensation or salary.

It was said about him that he would not waste any moment of the day or night but he would spend it busy with attaining knowledge. Even when he is walking in the streets, he will be busy going over what he had remembered and reviewing his notes.

His reputation and excellence as a scholar began to be recognised by the scholars and inhabitants of Damascus. His pursuit of knowledge dominated his entire life. He would put all of his time into studying, learning and teaching. It is even stated that he would not sleep except when sleep would overtake him. He would rest on his book and sleep for a little, then he would act startled upon awakening and continue studying. He once said about himself, "I spent two years without lying on the ground [to sleep] on my side."

4 Al-Muhadh-dhab is the book compiled by Imam al-Shīrāzi, which was explained partially by Imam al-Nawawī. It is a book in comparative fiqh

His Austerity

He led a very austere, simple and modest life although it would have been possible for him to live otherwise, given his teaching position and influence. Some narrations state that all the clothing he possessed was a turban and a long gown. He did not desire any of the pleasures of this world. At one point in time, he would not eat anything except some cake and olives that his father would send him from time to time. One of the reasons for this was that he was certain that such food came from permissible sources. He had a similar attitude to fruit, as he was certain that a lot of fruit was coming from endowment properties; and were not supposed to be handed out. The other reason for not eating fruit was his understanding that fruit made his body moist and thence: overtaken by sleep and tire.

He did not accept a stipend for his teaching, and his only material possessions of this world were books as his small room was like a warehouse of books and his goal was not simply to possess a large library. His books were not for decoration or display. Instead, he benefited greatly from those works and, from his lectures and writings, numerous people have benefited from them since then.

Al-Nawawī never married

Al-Nawawī never got married and the reasons for this was his desire for knowledge and disinterest in pleasures of this world. His life was filled with the desire to learn, teach and engage in acts of worship. Some say that he did not marry because he feared that he would not be able to fulfil the rights of his wife due to his learning desires.

His Writings/Books

Al-Nawawī started writing in the year 663. Hence, in a span of twelve or thirteen years, he compiled some of the most important works in the history of Islam.

Some of his works that he completed in that short time, include:

1 - Riyāḍ al-Sāliḥīn (Gardens of the Righteous)

2 - Al-Minhāj fī Sharḥ Ṣaḥīḥ Muslim (His Commentary to Sahih Muslim)

3 - Al-Majmū' Sharḥ al-Muhadh-dhab

4 - Minhāj al-Tālibīn (The Path of the Seekers)

5 - Tahdhīb al-'Asmā' wa al-Lughāt (Abridgement of the Names and Dialects)

6 - Forty Aḥadīth

7 - Kitāb al-Adhkār (Book of Remembrances)

8 - Tabaqāt al-Shāfi'iyyah (The Levels of the Shāfi'ī scholars)

9 - Rawḍat al- Tālibīn (Garden of the Seekers)

10 - Bustān al-'Ārifīn (Garden of the Aware)

11 - Al-Tibyān fī Ādāb Ḥamalat al-Quran (The Explanation of the etiquette of the carriers of the Quran)

Al-Nawawī and the Ruler

The leader of the Muslims during much of al-Nawawī's lifetime was al-Sultān al-Ẓāhir. He was the one who fought off the Mongols and handed them a great defeat. However, his status and popularity did not prevent al-Nawawī from standing up to him when he was wrong. On more than one occasion, al-Nawawī either approached the ruler in the Hall of Justice or sent him letters concerning a particular matter that was of common interest to the people of Damascus.

On one occasion, al-Nawawī sent the Sultan a letter on behalf of the Muslim masses, co-signed by a number of other scholars. This letter was a request for the ruler to lessen the taxes that were placed on the inhabitants of Shām. The Intention of al-Nawawī's letter was about correcting the wrong that was being done by the ruler. He did not bow down to the ruler, just because he was the ruler and just because he had done some excellent deeds in the past. However, he realised that he must advise him to what's right. In that response, the ruler claimed that he needed to collect those taxes for the sake of *jihād*.

On his continuous encounters with the ruler through letters and his personal persuasion to urge the ruler for all the right reasons, the ruler became very upset with al-Nawawī. Hence, he decided to have him removed from Damascus. Al-Nawawī said that he would listen and obey- perhaps realising that such would cause less harm and civil strife then remaining in Damascus and opposing the ruler.

He commented: "As for myself, threats do not harm me or mean anything to me. They will not keep me from advising the ruler, for I believe that this is obligatory upon me and others."

Hence, he left Damascus and went to his hometown of Nawā. Scholars of that time went to try to bring al-Nawawī back to Damascus. However, he refused. He said that he would not enter Damascus if al-Ẓāhir was still there. After a few months, al-Ẓāhir Baibars died.

His Death

After returning to Nawā, al-Nawawī fell ill and passed away. He died on the 24th of Rajab, 676 AH (1277 AD). He died at the age of forty-five. However, by the grace and mercy of Allah, his accomplishments during his short life span were equal to or greater than many who lived even twice as long as he did.

When the news of his death reached Damascus, the people were very saddened. Tears flowed from their eyes. One of the greatest scholars and greatest leaders of the people had passed away. Indeed, one who was greatly beloved by almost everyone he touched in his life had died.

His Burial Place

Al-Nawawī was buried in his hometown of Nawā, Syria. He wished and advised that his grave would be according to the Sunnah (i.e. to be levelled and not prominent). However, some people decided to build a dome over his grave. However, Allah willed that al-Nawawī's wish be fulfilled. Every time they tried to build something over his grave, it was destroyed. His grave, after many attempts, was finally left flat, slightly marked and according to the sunnah. His grave is still well-known and recognised today. However, it is despicable that in 2015, extremists chose to blow up his grave.

May Allah reward this great man, a giant by all accounts for his efforts and striving for the sake of Allah.

01

The Author's Introduction - may Allah Almighty have mercy on him

Praise be to Allah, the One, the Subjugator, the Mighty, the All-Forgiving. The One who has determined the destinies, who directs affairs. He wraps the night over the day, as an insight for those who have hearts and vision.

It is He who awakens from His creation those whom He has chosen, and thus admits them amongst the good folk. It is He who has aided with guidance those He has chosen of His slaves, and thus made them of the righteous. He has given to those whom He loves insight into the realities, such that He made them abstinent in regards to this abode; and such that they have strived for His pleasure and to prepare for the Permanent Abode[5]; and to avoid that which angers Him and to safeguard from the torment of the Fire.

I praise Him the most eloquent of praises for all His blessings, and I ask him more of His virtue and generosity. I bear witness that there is no God but Allah in recognition of His Oneness, and in affirmation of what is obligatory on all creation to submit to with regards to His Lordship.

5 Meaning the dwelling in Paradise in the Next Life

I bear witness that Muhammad is His slave and Messenger, and His chosen beloved one from His creation. He is the most honoured of all Allah's creation, from the first till the last. He is the most noble of creation, most pure and most complete. He is the most aware among them in regards to Allah – the Exalted; and the most fearing of Him. He is the most knowledgeable amongst them of Him and the most pious. He is the most intense in his strive towards Him and in his worship, fear and ascetism. He is the mightiest in his morals, and most extensive in his gentleness and compassion towards the believers.

Prayers and greetings of Allah be upon him and upon the Prophets, and their families and their entire companions, and those who follow them with righteousness until the Day of Accounting; whenever he is mentioned by those who remember him; and whenever the heedless are distracted from his mention.

As for then; The *dunyā* is an abode of depletion, not an abode of eternity. It is [also] an abode of transit, not an abode of delight. It is an abode of cessation; not one of permanence. It is an abode of passing away, not an abode of continuity. What I have stated has been reinforced with well-grounded rationale as well as proofs which are decisive in their transmission. It is something which the general public as well as the elite are equal in; the rich as well as the paupers. Senses and visual witnessing have both determined this, such that its clarity accepts no further increase in knowing:

If the day stands in need of proof
then nothing will be valid in [people's] minds

As the *dunyā* is in the format that I have aforementioned, and the exhortation that I gave; within the Holy Quran has come the warning against being dependent on it, being deceived by it or relying on it in a manner which is more known than to mention,

and more apparent than to be made further manifest.
Likewise, the Prophetic *aḥādīth* and wise traditions have also come to aid such warnings. Hence, the awake amongst its people are the extensive worshipers; and the wisest people in it are the ascetics.

[Of] The best description of the *Dunyā*

Look at the ruins how they have changed
After their inhabitants, and how they are unrecognisable.

The wear extended its trails over its demarcations
Such that its stones have tumbled down and shattered.

The groupings of its people have departed on their ways
Their news has disappeared and become concealed.

When I look - in reflection – about their dwellings
Teardrops drown out my eyelashes; and flow.

Had I been wiser, I would not have awoken from crying
Enough therein for my eyes, as what it has seen.

The *dunyā* has erected for us the beauty of its ornaments
Out of deception for us and treachery, never ceasing.

It is that which never tastes sweet in the mouth;
Even after the sweetness, its taste changes: becoming bitter.

Deceiving in its beauty as it comes forth
Causing grief with its end, as it departs.

A giver who strips away its gifts
Seeking to ruin that which it has constructed.

When it builds something for an owner of wealth
It erects its catapults on it, and as such, destroys it.

Someone else said:

When someone praises the *dunyā* for a pleasing life [he has]
By my life, soon he shall blame it when only little remains.

When it departs, it becomes regretful for the person
And when it comes forth, it comes with many troubling worries.

02

Clarification of what this book entails

If the aforementioned is understood, and what I have described is affirmed, then it is imperative on the human to take the path of the intellectuals, and to walk in the direction of those who have vision. We ask Allah – the Most Generous, Compassionate, All Merciful – to bestow on us that, and to guide us to the most directed of ways. And here I am commencing a book which enlightens us on taking the path that I have introduced, as a means to adopt the beautiful morals that I have described. In it, I will mention – with the will of Allah Exalted be He – sections of precious perspectives, and realities of concepts; and I spread this throughout the book, so that it would be less arduous for the one who observes, and closer to a reminder.

I do not restrict myself to organise it into chapters, as this will bring about boredom to the one who browses the book. I will mention – with the will of Allah the Exalted – of the noble verses, and Prophetic *aḥādīth*, enlightening sayings of the predecessors, and the virtuous traditions from the good folk which include stories as well as approved ascetic poems.

Mostly, I clarify the authenticity of the hadith and the condition of its narrators, and to explain what has hidden and is problematic in its meaning. I also identify what needs to be clear in order to avoid distortion and to escape alteration and misrepresentation. Then, I may mention what I mention with my chain of transmission, as it would be firmer in the readers' selves.

I may remove the chain for the sake of brevity, and to avoid elongation and replication; as this book was compiled for worshippers who are not in need of knowing the chains. Rather, they may dislike them in some instances, for it may give rise to boredom.

The majority of that which I narrate come – with the grace of Allah – with well-known chains, known in the apparent books which are widespread. Where the hadith or narration has a difficult word or phrase, then I would clarify it [using the appropriate vowel sounds]. Where there is need for explanation, I explain; and what may be prone to misunderstanding, I clarify.

Included in this book – with the will of Allah the Exalted – are subjects within the Islamic sciences, subtleties from hadith and *fiqh* and religious etiquette. There are also aspects of hadith science as well as hidden jurisprudential finer points. It also contains important issues of the *'aqīdah* principles, and resourceful precious rules, and subtle oddities, which are desirable to be mentioned and recommended to narrate in the congregations. Also included is the knowledge of the hearts, its diseases, medicine and treatment.

There may be certain things mentioned which need a more protracted explanation, but cannot be included in this book. In these instances, I will mention its intended purpose briefly, or I will refer to an extended explanation in a book of other scholars of vision and intellect. It may be that I will refer to a book of my own compilation; and my intention – with the will of Allah – is not to boast or brag; nor to show off my compilations or to increase their mention. It is rather to direct towards good, to signpost, and to explain where to find such explanations and provide a solid reference to this effect.

I am alerting to this specificity, because I saw of the people who fault the one who takes such a path, due to their ignorance towards him; mistrust, corruption, or out of envy, limitations or due to stubbornness. So, I wanted to establish this meaning in the mind of the reader for this compilation, such that he can cleanse his self from rotten suspicion and aggression.

I ask Allah the Most Generous, to guide me towards the best of intentions, and to provide aid for all the various acts of obedience, and to make them easy. As I ask Him for guidance to it, always and in perpetual increase until death.

As I ask Him all the above, for all whom I love and those who love me for Allah – the Exalted; and for all the Muslims – male and female; and that He gathers us in the abode of His Generosity in the highest of stations, and that He bestows on us His pleasure, as well as all types of goodness.

How great is that which Allah has willed. I grasp on to Allah, I seek help of Allah, I depend on Allah. There is no strength or ability to move except with Allah, Most High and Mighty. Enough for us is Allah, and He is the best to depend on.

O Allah, I ask you with every means, and I intercede to you with all intercessions, to greatly and extensively benefit me – with this book – as well as my beloved, and all Muslims, O You Who is incapacitated by none; and nothing is too great for You!
And this introduction outlines the purpose of this book.

03

Sincerity (Ikhlāṣ) and having a conscious intention in all actions – outward and inward

Allah says:

﴿وَمَا أُمِرُوا إِلاّ لِيَعبُدُوا اللهَ مُخلِصِينَ لَهُ الدِّينَ حُنَفاءَ وَيُقِيمُوا الصَّلَوٰةَ وَيُؤتُوا الزَّكَوٰةَ وَذَٰلِكَ دِينُ القَيِّمَةِ﴾

﴿They were only ordered to worship Allah, making their *dīn* sincerely to Him, as people of pure natural belief, and to establish *salah* and pay *zakah* - that is the upright *dīn*.﴾[6]

This means the straight (*mustaqīm*) system of worship. It is also said that it means "the upright nation"; and it has also been said: "that which is established on the truth", and Allah knows best.

And Allah said:

﴿وَمَن يَخرُج مِن بَيتِهِ مُهَاجِراً إِلى اللهِ وَرَسُولِهِ ثُمَّ يُدرِكهُ المَوتُ فَقَد وَقَعَ أَجرُهُ عَلَى اللهِ﴾

﴿And whoever leaves his home, emigrating to Allah and His Messenger, and death catches up with him, then his reward has become established with Allah.﴾[7]

6 Holy Quran: Chapter of the Clear Proof 98:5
7 Holy Quran: Chapter of the Women 4:100

And Allah said:

﴿رَبُّكُم أَعلَمُ بِمَا فِي نُفُوسِكُم﴾

﴿Your Lord knows best what is in your selves.﴾[8]

Allah says:

﴿لَن يَنالَ اللهَ لُحُومُها وَلَا دِماؤُها وَلَكِن يَنالُهُ التَّقوَى مِنكُمْ﴾

﴿Its[9] flesh and blood does not reach Allah, rather your piety (*tawqā*) is what reaches Him.﴾[10]

Ibn 'Abbās ﷺ said, "It means that your intentions reach Him."

'Ibrāhīm said, "*Taqwā* is the means by which you desire Him."

Imam Abu al-Ḥasan al-Wāḥidī reported that al-Zajjāj said, "The meaning of this is that Allah will not accept an offering of flesh and blood when it is offered without fearful awareness of Allah. He accepts that through which you show Him your fearful awareness of Him."

The above [references] indicate that no act of worship is without intention. The intention is that you want to draw near to Allah and carry out His command.

Our Shaykh the Imam Hadith Master Abu al-Baqā' Khalid ibn Yūsuf ibn Sa'īd ibn al-Ḥasan ibn al-Mufarraj ibn Bikār al-Maqdisī al-Nābulsī al-Shāfi'ī ﷺ informed us saying that Abu al-Yamān al-Kindī informed us that Muhammad ibn Abdul Bāqī al-'Anṣārī informed us that Abu Muhammad al-Ḥasan ibn 'Alī al-Jawharī informed us that Hadith Master Abu al-Ḥusayn al-Muẓaffar informed us that Abu Bakr Muhammad ibn Muhammad ibn Sulaymān al-Wāsitī informed us that Abu Nu'aym 'Abd ibn

8 Holy Quran: Chapter of the Night Journey 17:25
9 That of the sacrificed animal
10 Holy Quran: Chapter of Hajj 22:37

Hishām al-Ḥalabī narrated to us from Ibn al-Mubarāk from Yaḥyā ibn Sa'īd from Muhammad ibn 'Ibrāhīm at-Taymī from 'Alqamah ibn Waqqāṣ al-Laythī that 'Omar ibn al-Khattāb ☙ said that the Messenger of Allah 🌸 said:

"Indeed, actions are only by intentions. And every person shall only get what they intend. Therefore, whoever's migration is to Allah and His Messenger, then his migration is to Allah and His Messenger. And, whoever's migration is to gain something of this *dunyā* or to marry a woman, then his migration is for that for which he migrated."

This hadith is unanimously agreed to be sound. Its position is immense and sublime. It is one of the foundations of belief (*īmān*), its first pillar and its strongest support.

It is a singular and unique from one consideration; and a famous well-known from another consideration.
The backbone of its *isnād* is Yaḥyā ibn Sa'īd al-'Anṣārī.

The Hadith Masters said, "This hadith from the Prophet 🌸 is only authentic from the path of 'Omar ibn al-Khattāb. And it is only correctly transmitted via the way of 'Alqamah. And from 'Alqamah: only via 'Ibrāhīm ibn Muhammad al-Taymī. And from 'Ibrāhīm by way of Yaḥyā ibn Sa'īd. From Yaḥyā, the transmission of it spreads out to more than 200 people, most of whom are Imams."

Imam Abu AbdUllah Muhammad ibn Ismā'īl al-Bukhārī (may Allah have mercy on him) related it in his *Ṣaḥīḥ* in seven places. He related it at the beginning of his book, and in the chapters on *īmān*, marriage, freeing slaves, migration, giving up deceptions and in the chapter of the oaths.

This hadith is related in the *Ṣaḥīḥ* in various wordings:
"Indeed, actions are only by intentions."

The version which reads "Actions are by intentions" at the beginning of the Book of "*Al-Shihāb*" does not include the word (إنما); Abu Mūsā al-'Asbahānī said that its *isnād* is not *ṣaḥīḥ*.

The meaning of the intention is to aim for the goal. It is the heart's resolve.

"Indeed" (إنما) is used to express limitation. It affirms what is mentioned, and rejects everything else.

The meaning of the hadith is that the shari'a based actions are not correct except by intention. As for the one whose goal is the pleasure of Allah by his migration, and as for the one whose goal is this world, both of them obtain only that respective portion.

According to this hadith, 'intention' is a precondition for *wūdū'* as well as other acts, such as *ghusl*, *tayammum*, *salah*, *zakāh*, fasting, spiritual retreat, hajj and so on.

Our Imam Muhammad ibn 'Idrīs al-Shāfi'ī ﵁ said: "This hadith enters into seventy chapters of *fiqh*."

He also said, "This hadith is one third of knowledge."

Abu AbdUllah - Ahmad ibn Ḥanbal ﵁ stated, "It enters into a third of knowledge." Others have mentioned similar sayings to both of these Imams.

Imam Abu Bakr al-Bayhaqī said in the beginning of his book *'The Summary of the Sunan'*: "What al-Shāfi'ī ﵁ meant about the fact that it is a third of knowledge derives from the fact that the slave[11] acquires everything by means of his heart, his tongue and his intentions. The 'intention' is one of the divisions of his acquisition, yet it is the most predominant of the three, because it is an act of worship in its own merit. The other two are not. Words and actions can be perverted by showing-off. But this does not affect intention in any way."

Scholars ﷺ recommend that you begin all compilations with this hadith. Imam Abu AbdUllah al-Bukhārī (may Allah have mercy on him) is one such example of those who have begun their books with it. It is the first hadith in his *Ṣaḥīḥ* Collection, which is the most authentic book after the Book of Allah - Most Exalted.

We have been narrated to from Imam Abu Sa'īd Abdul Raḥmān ibn Mahdī (may Allah have mercy on him) who said, "If I had compiled a book, I would have started every chapter with this hadith."

We have also been narrated to from him, his saying, "Whoever wants to compile a book, let him begin it with this hadith."

We have been narrated to from Imam Abu Sulaymān Ḥamd ibn Muhammad ibn 'Ibrāhīm al-Khaṭṭābī, in that which I read in the beginning of his book "*Al-I'lām*" the commentary on Ṣaḥīḥ al-Bukhārī, he said, "Our foremost shaykhs recommended that we give precedence to this hadith, 'Indeed, actions are only by the intention' at the start of all matters of the *dīn* that are initiated or commenced; as it is generally needed in all aspects of the *dīn*."

Many more similar sayings have been conveyed to us from the early Predecessors ﷺ which demonstrate their concern with this hadith.

Of it: The chain of transmission (*isnād*) of this hadith is very rare and unique among the people of hadith. This is due to the fact

11 Slave refers to a person, as any person is the slave of Allah

that its chain of transmission includes three followers[12], each one relating the hadith from the other.

These three followers are: Yaḥyā ibn Sa'id al-'Anṣārī, Muhammad ibn 'Ibrāhīm al-Taymī and 'Alqamah ibn Waqqāṣ ﷺ

Although this is marvellous, there are several *ṣaḥīḥ aḥādīth* that have three followers relating the hadith from one another, and there are even some that include four followers in the chain. The Hadith Master Abdul Qādir al-Rahāwī (may Allah have mercy on him) has gathered them all together in a section of his book. I have transmitted it and condensed it at the beginning of my commentary on Ṣaḥīḥ al-Bukhārī. I added some others to them which I found to be like them, making them more than thirty *aḥādīth* of this kind, but Allah knows best.

12 Follower: someone who has met and studied with a companion of the Prophet ﷺ

04

The *aḥādīth* around which the Sphere of Islam rotates

Of the matters which necessitate special care is to express those *aḥadīth* which are said to be the basis of Islam and the roots of the *dīn*; or those around which Islam, *fiqh* or knowledge rotate. We will mention them in this section because one of them is the hadith, **"Indeed actions only go by intentions"**. They are very important, and should be the first to be dealt with.

Scholars have differed a great deal about their number. The Hadith Master and Imam Shaykh Abu 'Amr 'Othmān ibn Abdul Raḥmān (known as Ibn al-Ṣalāḥ) – may Allah have mercy on him – has exerted his effort to compile and highlight them. There can be no extension to his verification and precision.

I just convey what he has mentioned, as a condensed version; and I add to them some of what he has not mentioned, for *dīn* is sincerity.

Part of this sincerity is to attribute the unique benefit derived to the one who has said it. Whoever does that, then his knowledge and state would be blessed. As for he who deceives [others] into thinking that which he has taken of others' words are his[13], then it is befitting that others would not benefit from his knowledge, nor should he receive

13 Known as plagiarism

any blessing in his state. And the people of knowledge and virtue continue to ascribe benefits to the ones who said them. We ask Allah – Most Exalted – for assistance to do this always.

After weighing what the various Imams have said about which *aḥādīth* are central to Islam and after considering their disagreement about their number, and which *aḥādīth* they actually are, Shaykh Abu ʻAmr said: "I arrived at twenty-six *aḥādīth*."

01
First Hadith

"Indeed, actions are only by intentions...."

02
Second Hadith

From ʻĀ'ishah - may Allah be pleased with her – who said that the Messenger of Allah ﷺ said:
"If anyone innovates in this affair of ours which is not part of it, it is rejected."

This hadith is agreed upon being *ṣaḥīḥ*. It is narrated by al-Bukhārī and Muslim in their Ṣaḥīḥ collections. In the version for Muslim, it says:
"If anyone enacts an action which is not in accordance with this affair of ours..."

03
Third Hadith

From al-Nu'mān ibn Bashīr (may Allah be pleased with them both) who said, 'I heard the Messenger of Allah ﷺ say: **"The *halal* is clear and the *ḥarām* is clear. Between the two there are ambiguous matters about which most people have no knowledge. Whoever exercises caution with regard to what is ambiguous shows prudence in respect of his *dīn* and his honour. Whoever falls into the ambiguous things, falls into *ḥarām*. Like a shepherd who grazes [his flock] near a [protected] sanctuary, he is about to fall within it. Verily, every king has a sanctuary. Verily, the sanctuary of Allah are the things that He has made prohibited. Verily, there is a bitesize organ in the body; if it is sound, the entire body is sound. And where it would be corrupt, the entire body would be corrupt. Verily, it is the heart".'**

This hadith is agreed upon to be *ṣaḥīḥ*. We have had it narrated to us in the two Ṣaḥīḥ collections.

04
Fourth Hadith

From AbdUllah ibn Mas'ūd ﷺ who said, The Messenger of Allah ﷺ narrated to us – and he is the truthful and the affirmed one: **"The creation of any one of you is brought together in the womb of his mother for forty days as a sperm-drop. Then he would be a leech-like clot in the similar period. Then, he would be the size and shape of a bite in the similar period. Then an angel is sent to him and he breathes the spirit into him and is commanded with**

four words: to write down his provision, his life-span, his action, and whether he will be wretched or happy.

By Him who there is no God but He, one of you will enact the actions of someone destined for *al-Jannah*, until there is only an arm's length between him and it, and then what is written will overtake him and he will do the actions of someone destined for the Fire and will enter it.

And one of you will enact the actions of someone destined for the Fire until there is only an arm's length between him and it, and then what is written will overtake him and he will do the actions of someone destined for *al-Jannah* and will enter it."

Al-Bukhārī and Muslim narrated it in their Ṣaḥīḥ collections.

05
Fifth Hadith

Al-Ḥasan ibn 'Alī - may Allah be pleased with them both – said, "I memorised from the Messenger of Allah ﷺ:
"Abandon what gives you doubt for what gives you no doubt."

It is a *ṣaḥīḥ* hadith, narrated by Abu 'Isā al-Tirmidhī and Abu Abdul Raḥmān al-Nasā'ī. Abu 'Isā al-Tirmidhī said that it is a *ṣaḥīḥ* hadith.

06
Sixth Hadith

Abu Hurayrah ﷺ reported that the Messenger of Allah ﷺ said:
"Of the Excellence of one's Islam is his abandoning that which does not concern him."

It is a sound hadith: al-Tirmidhī and Ibn Mājah narrated it.

07
Seventh Hadith

Anas ibn Malik ﷺ said that the Prophet ﷺ said:
"Not one of you will believe until he loves for his brother what he loves for himself."

It is agreed to be *ṣaḥīḥ*.

08
Eighth Hadith

Abu Hurayrah ﷺ said, 'The Messenger of Allah ﷺ said:
"O People! Certainly, Allah is good and He only accepts that which is good. Allah has commanded the believers with that which He commanded the Messengers.

Allah Almighty says, 'O Messengers! Eat of the good things and do righteous [deeds]' and the Almighty says, 'O You who have believed! Eat of the good things We have provided for you.'"

Then he mentioned a man who goes on a long journey...

"is dishevelled and dusty, he stretches his arms to heaven, saying, 'O Lord! O Lord!'; yet his food is *ḥarām*, his drink is *ḥarām*, his clothes are *ḥarām*, and he is nourished by *ḥarām*: How could such a man be responded to?"

Narrated by Muslim in his Ṣaḥīḥ [collection].

09
Ninth Hadith

"There should be no harm or mutual harming."

Mālik narrated it as *mursal*[14]. Al-Dāraquṭnī and a group narrated it with an uninterrupted chain of transmission. It is a sound hadith.

10
Tenth Hadith

Tamīm al-Dārī ⬥ reported that the Prophet ⬥ said:
"Dīn is sincerity / faithfulness."
We asked: "To whom?"
He replied:
"To Allah; To His Messenger; and to the Imams of the Muslims, and their common people."

Narrated by Muslim.

---

14 A type of hadith transmission in which the name and person of the companion narrating from the Prophet ⬥ is missing in the chain

11
Eleventh Hadith

——•••◆•••——

Abu Hurayrah ☙ said that he heard the Prophet ﷺ say:
"What I have prohibited you from doing, then abstain from it. And what I have commanded you to do, then do as much as you can. For those before you were destroyed due to their excessive questioning and their disagreeing with their Prophets."
It is agreed to be *ṣaḥīḥ*.

12
Twelfth Hadith

——•••◆•••——

Sahl ibn Sa'ad ☙ said:
'A man came to the Messenger of Allah ﷺ and said: "O Messenger of Allah, show me an action which if I did, then Allah will love me and people will love me."
He replied:
"Abstain from the *dunyā*: Allah will love you. Do without what people have: people will love you!"

It is a sound hadith narrated by Ibn Mājah.

13
Thirteenth Hadith

——•••◆•••——

Ibn Mas'ūd ☙ reported that the Messenger of Allah ﷺ said:
"The blood of a Muslim who witnesses that there is no God except Allah and that I am the Messenger of Allah is not

lawful [to shed] except in three cases: a married person who commits adultery; a life for a life, and someone who abandons the *dīn* and splits away from the community."

It is agreed to be *ṣaḥīḥ*.

14
Fourteenth Hadith

AbdUllah ibn 'Omar (may Allah be pleased with them both) reported that the Messenger of Allah ﷺ said:
"I have been commanded to fight people until they testify that there is no God except Allah and Muhammad is the Messenger of Allah, establish *salah*, and pay *zakah*. If they do that, their lives and their property are protected from me, except for the right of Islam. Their reckoning is up to Allah Almighty."

It is agreed that it is *ṣaḥīḥ*.

15
Fifteenth Hadith

Ibn 'Omar (may Allah be pleased with them both) reported that the Messenger of Allah ﷺ said:
"Islam is based on five: the testimony that there is no God except Allah and that Muhammad is the Messenger of Allah; establishing *salah*, paying *zakah*, *hajj* and fasting *Ramadan*."

It is agreed that it is *ṣaḥīḥ*.

16
Sixteenth Hadith

Ibn ʻAbbās (may Allah be pleased with them both) reported that the Messenger of Allah ﷺ said:
"If people are to be given according to their claims [only]; then men would lay claim to the property of [other] people and to their blood. However, the one making the claim must bring clear proof, and the one who denies it must take an oath."

This is a sound hadith narrated by al-Bayhaqī with this wording, whilst part of it is included in the two Ṣaḥīḥ collections.

17
Seventeenth Hadith

Wābiṣah ibn Maʻbad ﷺ mentioned that he went to the Messenger of Allah ﷺ who said to him:
"Have you come to ask me about righteousness and sin?"
He said: "I replied: 'Yes'."
He said:
"Consult your heart. Righteousness is that which the soul is at rest with and the heart finds comfort therein. Sin is what itches in yourself, and resonates to and fro in your breast; even if people give you a decision, and then give you another."

One version has:
"even if those who issue fatwā, give you a fatwā."

It is a sound hadith narrated by Ahmad ibn Ḥanbal, al-Dārimī and others.

In the book of Ṣaḥīḥ Muslim, from the narration of al-Nawwās ibn Sam'ān ﵁ from the Prophet ﷺ who said:
"Righteousness is good character and sin is that which itches within yourself and which you hate people to observe it."

18
Eighteenth Hadith

Shaddād ibn 'Aws ﵁ reported that the Messenger of Allah ﷺ said:
"Allah has ordained excellence for everything. Therefore, when you kill, kill well. When you sacrifice, sacrifice well. Let one of you sharpen his knife and let him relieve his animal to be slaughtered."

Narrated by Muslim.

19
Nineteenth Hadith

Abu Hurayrah ﵁ reported that the Messenger of Allah ﷺ said:
"Whoever believes in Allah and the Final Day, let him speak what is good or remain silent. Whoever believes in Allah and the Final Day should honour his neighbour. Whoever believes in Allah and the Final Day should honour his guest."

It is agreed to be *ṣaḥīḥ*.

20
Twentieth Hadith

Abu Hurayrah ﵁ reported that a man said to the Prophet ﷺ:
"Advise me!"
He said:
"Do not get angry."
He repeated his request several times, and the Prophet repeated:
"Do not get angry."

Al-Bukhārī narrated it in his Ṣaḥīḥ collection.

21
Twenty-First Hadith

Abu Tha'labah ﵁ reported that the Messenger of Allah ﷺ said:
"Allah has obliged obligations, so you should not neglect them! He has placed limits, so you should not transgress them! He has prohibited matters, so you should not violate them. And He has been silent about certain things as a mercy to you – not out of forgetfulness – so do not seek them!"

Al-Daraqutnī narrated it with a sound chain of transmission.

22
Twenty-Second Hadith

Abu Dharr and Mu'ādh (may Allah be pleased with them both) reported that the Messenger of Allah ﷺ said:
"Fear Allah wherever [and however] you are. Follow up an evil action with a good action, it will wipe it out; and treat people well."

Al-Tirmidhī narrated it and said that it is a sound hadith. In some verified copies, he says that it is a sound *ṣaḥīḥ* hadith.

23
Twenty-Third Hadith

Mu'ādh ﷺ narrated saying: 'I said, "O Messenger of Allah, inform me of an action I can do which will admit me to *al-Jannah* and keep me far away from the Fire!'
He said:
"You have asked about a great matter, but it is easy for the one to whom Allah makes it easy. You should worship Allah and do not associate anything with Him; and establish *salah*, pay *zakah*, fast *Ramadan* and perform *hajj* to the House."

Then he said:
"Shall I direct you to the gates of good? Fasting is a shield. Charity extinguishes the sin as water extinguishes fire. The *salah* of a person in the middle of the night."

Then he recited:

﴿تَتَجافَى جُنُوبُهم عن المَضاجع يَدعُونَ ربَّهم خَوفاً وَطَمعاً، وممّا رزقناهم ينفقون
فَلا تعلَمُ نفسٌ ما أُخفيَ لَهُم من قُرَّةِ أعين، جزاءً بما كانوا يعملون﴾.

﴿Their sides eschew their beds as they call on their Lord in fear and out of hope. And they give of what We have provided them. No self knows the delight that is hidden away for it in recompense for what it used to do.﴾

Then he said:
"Shall I tell you of the head of the matter, its backbone and its utmost peak?"
I said: "Yes indeed, Messenger of Allah."
He said:
"The head of the matter is Islam and its backbone is *salah*; and its utmost peak is *jihād*."
Then he said:
"Shall I tell you of the purpose of all that?"
I said: "Yes, Messenger of Allah."
He took hold of his tongue and said:
"Restrain this!"
I said, "Messenger of Allah, will we be taken to task for what we say?"
He said:
"May your mother be bereaved of you! What else will cause people to be thrown on their faces in the Fire other than the harvests of their tongues?"

Al-Tirmidhī narrated it and said it is a sound *ṣaḥīḥ* hadith.

24
Twenty-Fourth Hadith

From al-'Irbāḍ ibn Sāriyah ⁓ who said:
"The Messenger of Allah ⁓ gave us a profound exhortation which brought fear to the hearts afraid and made the eyes weep. We said, 'O Messenger of Allah, it is an exhortation which seems to be a farewell one, so advise us!'

He said:
'I commend you to fear Allah; and to hear and obey, even if a slave takes command over you. For those who live on, shall see much disagreement. So, you must hold on to my *Sunnah* and the *sunnah* of the rightly-guided successors, who come after me. Bite onto it with your teeth. And beware of innovated matters, for every *bid'ah* is misguidance'."

Narrated by Abū Dāwūd and al-Tirmidhī who said that it is a sound *ṣaḥīḥ* hadith.

25
Twenty-Fifth Hadith

It has been narrated that Ibn 'Abbās – may Allah be pleased with them both – said:

"I was behind the Prophet ⁓ one day when he said:
'O Young boy, I will teach you some words:
Guard Allah, He will guard you!
Guard Allah, you will find Him before you!
If you ask, ask of Allah. If you seek help, seek help from Allah.

Know that even if the people were to join together to do something to benefit you, they could only benefit you in what Allah has written for you.
And if they were to join together to do something to harm you, they would not harm you except in what Allah has written for you.
The pens have been lifted and the pages have dried'."

Al-Tirmidhī narrated it and said that it is a sound *ṣaḥīḥ* hadith.

In a source other than al-Tirmidhī, a variation of this hadith reads:
"Guard Allah, you will find Him before you!
Be acquainted with Allah during ease, He will be acquainted with you during hardship.
Know that what has missed you could not have hit you; and that what hit you could not have missed you!"

and towards the end:
"Know that victory comes with patience, and relief comes with trouble; and that with hardship there is ease."

26
Twenty-Sixth Hadith

The hadith of Ibn 'Omar from his father 'Omar ibn al-Khattāb (may Allah be pleased with them both) in regards to belief in *Qadar*, articulation of *īmān*, Islam and *'iḥsān*, and the mentioning of the signs of the Day of Resurrection...

These are the *aḥadīth* which Shaykh Abu 'Amr ibn al-Ṣalāḥ - may Allah have mercy on him - mentioned. And further to this, and with similar meanings are:

27

Twenty-Seventh Hadith

From the authority of Sufyān ibn AbdUllah ﷺ who reported:
"I said, 'Messenger of Allah, tell me something about Islam which I could not ask from anyone but you!'
He said:
'Say: "I have believed in Allah" and then be straight/upright".'

Narrated by Muslim.

28

Twenty-Eighth Hadith

From Abu Mas'ūd al-Badrī 'Uqbah ibn 'Omar ﷺ who said:
"The Prophet ﷺ said:
'If you have no shame, do as you wish!'
Narrated by al-Bukhārī in his Ṣaḥīḥ Collection.

29

Twenty-Ninth Hadith

From Jābir ﷺ who said that a man asked the Prophet ﷺ, 'Do you see that if I pray the five prescribed prayers, fast Ramadan, make *halal* what is *halal* and make *ḥarām* what is *ḥarām*, and do not do anything more than that, will I enter *al-Jannah*?'

He said: **'Yes.'**

Narrated by Muslim.

05

The Reality of Ikhlāṣ and Truthfulness

As for *ikhlāṣ*, then Allah – Exalted be He – said:

﴿وَمَا أُمِرُوا إِلَّا لِيَعْبُدُوا اللهَ مُخْلِصِينَ لَهُ الدِّينَ﴾

﴾And they were not commanded except to worship Allah, sincere to Him in their *dīn*.﴿[15]

We have been narrated to from Hudhayfah ibn al-Yamān (may Allah be pleased with them both) who said: "I asked the Messenger of Allah ﷺ about Ikhlāṣ; what is it?
He said:
"I asked Jibrīl about *ikhlāṣ*; what is it?"
He said:
"I asked the Lord of Might about *ikhlāṣ*; what is it?"
He said:
"It is a treasure from My secrets which I safely place in the heart of whom I love of My slaves."

We have been narrated to from 'Ustādh Imam Abu al-Qāsim al-Qushayrī (may Allah have mercy on him) who said: "*Ikhlāṣ* is to single out the Truth [Allah] in obedience with resolve. It is

15 Holy Quran: Chapter of the Clear Proof 98:5

when one intends with one's obedience to come close to Allah the Exalted, despite anything beneath that of flattery for the sake of a creature; or to attain praise with people; or to be awarded commendation from the creation, or any meaning other than proximity to Allah, the Exalted."

He said: "And it is correct to say: *Ikhlāṣ* is to beware of the observation of people."

We have been narrated to from 'Ustādh Abu 'Alī al-Daqqāq (may Allah have mercy on him) who said, "*Ikhlāṣ* is to beware the observation of the creation. Truthfulness is the cleansing from the noticing of the self. Thus, the sincere person has no showing off; and the truthful has no admiration for oneself."

We have been narrated to from Abu Ya'qūb al-Sūsī ﷺ who said, 'Whenever they observe in their "sincerity" that they have Sincerity, then their "sincerity" is in need of Sincerity!'

We have been narrated to from the Noble Master Dhu al-Nūn al-Miṣrī ﷺ who said: "Three [things] are from the signs of *ikhlāṣ*:
1 - Praise and disparage from the general people are the same.
2 - To forget to see the actions in the actions.
3 - Seeking the reward of the action in the Hereafter."

From Abu 'Othmān al-Mughrabī (may Allah have mercy on him) who said: "*Ikhlāṣ* is forgetting to regard the creation by constantly regarding the Creator."

From Hudhayfah al-Mar'ashī (may Allah have mercy on him) who said: "*Ikhlāṣ* is that the slave's actions outwardly and inwardly are equal."

From the Noble Master Fuḍayl ibn 'Iyāḍ (may Allah have mercy on him) who said: "Leaving an action for the sake of people is showing off. Doing an action for the sake of mankind is *shirk* (associating with Allah). *Ikhlāṣ* is that Allah protects you from both."

The Noble Master Abu Muhammad Sahl ibn AbdUllah al-Tustarī (may Allah have mercy on him) was asked: "What is the most difficult thing on the *nafs* (self)?"
He said: "*Ikhlāṣ*; as there is no share for it, within it."

From Yūsuf ibn al-Ḥusayn (may Allah have mercy on him) who said: "The most magnificent thing in this life is *ikhlāṣ*."

From Abu 'Othmān al-Mughrabī (may Allah have mercy on him) who said, "The *ikhlāṣ* of the common people is that which the self has no share in. The *ikhlāṣ* of the elite is what is bestowed on them not [what happens] by them. Acts of obedience appear from them while they are cut off from them. They do not 'look' at them, nor do they reckon them."

We have been narrated to from the Noble Master the Follower Imam Makḥūl ﷺ that he said: "There is no slave[16] that is sincere for forty days except that the springs of wisdom appear from his heart and tongue."

We have been narrated to from Sahl al-Tustarī (may Allah have mercy on him) who said, "Whoever abstains from the *dunyā* for forty days, truthful and sincere from his heart, then the gifts[17] will appear for him. And for whomever they don't appear, then he has been denied truthfulness in his abstinence."

16 The word "slave" refers to a person as he/she are slaves of Allah
17 The actual word is "karāmāt" which we will explain later on

It was said to Sahl at-Tustarī, "How do the noble gifts appear for a person?"

He said, "He takes what he wants, as he wants and from wherever he wants."

Sahl al-Tustarī (may Allah have mercy on him) said: "The intellectuals looked into the definition of *ikhlāṣ*; and they did not find anything[18] other than this: 'That one's movement and stillness in private and in public is for Allah, The Exalted, alone. The self, nor the desire, nor the world are mingled with it."

Al-Sarī (may Allah have mercy on him) said: "Don't do anything for [the sake of] people, nor leave anything for their sake, nor give anything for their sake and don't reveal anything for their sake."

18 Meaning anything more succinct

06

Truthfulness

As for truthfulness, Allah – the Exalted said:

﴿يَـٰٓأَيُّهَا ٱلَّذِينَ ءَامَنُوا۟ ٱتَّقُوا۟ ٱللَّهَ وَكُونُوا۟ مَعَ ٱلصَّـٰدِقِينَ﴾

﴾O you who have believed, fear Allah and be with the truthful﴿[19]

We have been narrated to from the authority of 'Ustādh al-Qushayrī (may Allah have mercy on him) who said: "Truth is the pillar of the matter; and with it: lies its completeness; and in it: is its order."

He [also] said: "The least [level of] honesty is the equality of the private and the public."

We have been narrated to from Sahl (may Allah Almighty have mercy on him) who said: "The fragrance of honesty will not be smelt by a slave who has flattered himself or others."

We have been narrated to from Dhu al-Nūn (may Allah have mercy on him) that he said: "Truth is the sword of Allah, and it is not placed on anything, without cutting it."

We have been narrated to from the Glorious Master, the knowledgeable

19 Holy Quran: Chapter of Repentance 9:119

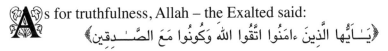

Imam al-Ḥārith al-Muḥāsabī (may Allah Almighty have mercy on him) who said: "The truthful is the one who does not care if all of his reputation goes out of the hearts of the creation for the sake of the goodness of his own heart. He does not like to inform people about [even] an ant's eggs' weight of his good work. He doesn't dislike that people notice the bad aspects of his actions, for his dislike is evidence that he loves the increase with them; and this is not the sincerity of those who are truthful."

And it was said: "If you ask Allah (Exalted be He) for honesty, He will award you a mirror in which you can see everything from the wonders of the *dunyā* and the Hereafter."

We have been narrated to from the Noble Master Abu al-Qāsim al-Junayd (may Allah be pleased with him) who said: "The truthful one fluctuates forty times a day, and the hypocrite [show-off] is static in one state for forty years."

I said[20] that its meaning is that the sincere person revolves with the truth however it is. Such that, if he saw the legal merit in a matter, then he will do it, even if that goes against his usual practice. And if he is presented with something more important in the shari'a, and he cannot combine between two practices, he goes towards the better; and his [fluctuate] state remains like that. It may be in one day, he has one hundred states, or a thousand or more, depending on his capability in the knowledge and the appearance [for him] of the minute details and points of wonder.

As for the hypocrite, then he adheres to one state; such that if an important proposition is presented to him, which is favoured by the shari'a, he does not carry out this important task. Rather, he maintains his condition because he shows off his worship and his affair to the creatures. He fears that in change, their love for him

20 Meaning Imam al-Nawawi

would dissipate; and thus, he maintains its continuation. Whereas, the truthful intends with his worship: Allah – Exalted be He. So, as soon as the shari'a favours a state, he will go towards it; and does not look to the creation.

I have simplified the statement in explaining this narration in the beginning of the explanation of *"al-Muhadh-dhab"*[21], and I mentioned its evidence and clarified it with examples. Its summary is what I have mentioned here, so I will confine it to that; and Allah knows best.

21 Al-Muhadh-dhab is the book compiled by Imam al-Shīrāzi, which was explained partially by Imam al-Nawawī'. It is a book in comparative fiqh

07

Recalling the intention in matters of obedience

Know that it is imperative for whomsoever wishes to do any act of obedience, even if small, to recall the intention; and that is to intend with his action, the pleasure of Allah the Almighty, and that his intention is done during the act.

This includes all acts of worship such as *salāh*, *fasting*, *wūḍū*, *tayammum*, *'i'tikāf*, *hajj*, *zakāh*, charity, fulfilling [others'] needs, visiting the sick, following the funerals, initiating *salām* and replying to it, blessing the one who has sneezed, denying evil, commanding the good, answering the invitation, and attending the gatherings of knowledge and remembrance; visiting the good people, spending on the family as well as the guest, honouring the people of affection, and the relatives; the study of knowledge, glancing through it, revising, teaching, reading, writing and compiling it; and fatwas, as well as what is similar to these acts. Even if he should eat, drink, or sleep, to intend the strength for the act of obedience to Allah, or to rest the body to give it energy for obedience.

Even if he wants to make love to his wife, he should intend on delivering her right to her, to conceive a righteous child who worships Allah – Exalted be He, and to protect himself, and to maintain it from aspirating towards *ḥarām* or the thought of it.

For he who is denied the intention in these acts, has been deprived of great good. As for he who has been guided to it, then he has been awarded substantial benefits. We therefore, ask Allah – Most Generous to help us for that, as well as towards all facets of good.

The evidence of this rule is what we have aforementioned of his saying ﷺ:
"Actions are but by intentions; and every person shall only get what he intended."

The Sayings of Scholars in regards to Intention

The scholars of language, principles and *fiqh* have said that the word (إنما) is used for restriction: affirming what has been stated and denying all other aspects; and we have previously mentioned this in the first section. They have said that the bestial acts are those done without intention.

We have been narrated to from the Noble Imam - whose status as an Imam, his nobility, majesty and mastery is agreed upon: Abu Yaḥyā Ḥabīb ibn Abi Thābit the follower, and the reliable amongst them[22] (may Allah have mercy on him).
It was said to him: "Tell us about the most difficult thing?"
He said: "Until the intention comes." or "The coming of the intention."

Sufyān al-Thawrī (may Allah have mercy on him) said: "I haven't dealt with anything more intense than my intention."

Yazīd ibn Hārūn (may Allah have mercy on him) said: "The intention has not become precious [or rare] in the hadith, except for its nobility."

22 i.e. the Followers, who are the students of the Companions of the Prophet ﷺ. A Follower is someone who has met and studied with at least one companion

Ibn 'Abbās ﵄ said: "A person is preserved in accordance to the value of his intention."

Others have said: "People are given in accordance with their intentions."

From Imam Abu AbdUllah Muhammad ibn 'Idrīs al-Shāfi'ī ﵁ – via a sound transmission - that he said: "I wished that the creation learnt this knowledge, without even a letter being ascribed to me."

Al-Shāfi'ī ﵁ – also said: "I have never debated with anyone for the purpose of defeating him. And when I debate with another, I would wish if the truth is manifest on his hands."

He also said: "I have never spoken to anyone, except I wished for him to be guided, made correct and aided, and that he would have the care of Allah Almighty and His preservation."

Imam Abu Yūsuf, the companion of Abu Ḥanīfah (may Allah have mercy on them both) said: "Seek Allah (Exalted be He) with your knowledge. For I have never sat in a gathering in which I intend to be humble, without getting up having risen above them. Nor did I sit in a gathering in which I intended to rise above them, without being shamed, before departing."

08

The Recording of Good deeds and Bad deeds

It has been established in the *ṣaḥīḥ aḥadīth* that the Messenger of Allah ﷺ said:
"Truly, Allah has recorded the good deeds and the bad deeds. Such that whoever is concerned with a good deed, but does not do it, Allah will record it with Him as a complete good deed. And if one is concerned with it; and enacts it, Allah will record it as [anything from] ten good deeds up to seven hundred times to manifold multiples."

It has also been established in the *ṣaḥīḥ* [hadith] that the Messenger of Allah ﷺ said in regards to the army that intends the *Ka'bah*:
"They will be quaked: from their first till their last."

'Ā'ishah (may Allah be pleased with her) asked: "O Messenger of Allah! How will their first till their last be quaked, and amongst them are the nobles and those who are not of them?"

He ﷺ said:
"They will be quaked: from their first till their last, then they will be resurrected according to their intentions."

It has been established in the two *Ṣaḥīḥ* books from Ibn 'Abbās (may Allah be pleased with them both) that the Messenger of Allah ﷺ said:
"There is no migration after the conquest. Rather it is *jihād* with intention."

I said: our companions and others have differed regarding the meaning of "No *hijrah* after the conquest". It was said that it means no migration from Makkah, as it has become an abode of Islam. It was also said that there is no migration – complete in virtue – after the conquest, as it was before the conquest.

As for the migration from the abode of the disbelievers today, then it is an emphasised obligation for whoever has the ability to do so, as one will not be able to manifest the *dīn* of Islam there. However, if one can manifest, then it is recommended and not obligatory; and Allah – the Most Exalted – knows best.

We have been narrated to from the Noble Master Abu Maysarah 'Omar ibn Sharḥabīl the Kufan follower al-Hamdānī - that if he took his wage, he would give of it in charity. When he would return to his family, and they would count his wages, they would find it the same.[23]
So, he said to his nephew: "Why don't you also do like this?"
They said: "If we knew that it would not decrease, we would have done so!"
Abu Maysarah said: "I am not stipulating this for my Lord – Honoured and Graced."

Our Imam Abu AbdUllah Muhammad ibn 'Idrīs al-Shafi'ī said: "The best of the *dunyā* and the hereafter are in [practicing] five qualities:
1 - The enrichment of the soul

23 Meaning it hasn't decreased from the charity given

2 - Averting harm
3 - Earning halal
4 - The dress of piety; and
5 - Trust in Allah ﷻ in all situations.

We have been narrated to from the authority of the Noble Master Ḥammād ibn Salamah (may Allah Almighty have mercy on him) and he was considered one of the *'abdāl*[24] who said, "Whoever seeks hadith for other than Allah, he will be deluded."

The Noble Master Ahmad ibn Abi al-Ḥawārī said in his book al-Zuhd, which he compiled, and you will see what I will convey of the precious things – *in sha Allah*. The chain of transmission to him has not yet come to me, yet. However, I do have an accurate copy, which some of the people of knowledge and expertise have told me that it is in the handwriting of al-Dāraqutnī - may Allah have mercy on him.

Ahmad said: Isḥāq ibn Khalaf told us saying: Ḥafṣ ibn Ghayāth told us, he said: "Abdul Raḥmān ibn al-Aswad did not used to eat bread except with an intention."
I said to Isḥāq: "And what is the intention in eating bread?"
He said: "He used to eat. When he felt burdensome for prayer, he would reduce [his intake], so that he would be light for it. Then, as he reduced [his intake], he would weaken, then he would start eating to gain strength. So, he ate it for that and abstained from it for that."

I said that the meaning of "being light" means that he has energy, and it [*salah*] is facilitated for him, such that he finds enjoyment in it.

Ahmad ibn Abi al-Ḥawārī: is either pronounced **al-Ḥawara** or **al-Ḥawārī**; the latter of which is more famous. However, I have

24 Translated as "replaceables" they are an elite group of righteous people, who replace one another. It is said that the world will not be void of any one of them at any one time. The notion of their existence is based on a hadith, which the hadith verifiers have disagreed on its authenticity

heard **al-Ḥawara** several times from our Shaykh the Hadith Master Abi al-Baqā' who narrates it from the people of precision or some of them; and Allah Almighty knows best.
Ahmad ibn Abi al-Ḥawārī said: "I heard Aba Sulaymān [al-Dārānī] (may Allah have mercy on him) say, 'Deal with Allah through your hearts'."

I said that this means cleanse your heart, purify and tame it; and don't interweave it with any of the outward actions.

Al-Dārānī is said as either **al-Dārānī** or **al-Dārā'ī**, with the "n" version being more prevalent. Both versions have been mentioned by Abu Sa'īd al-Sam'ānī in his book on Genealogy.[25] The "n" is more prevalent and widely used, while the "a" is closer to the origins.

He is attributed to a place called: Dāriyā, which is a large valued village near Damascus.

Abu Sulaymān was one of the outstanding gnostics, and of those who had outward *karāmāt* and astonishing states and apparent wisdoms. His name is Abdul Raḥmān ibn Ahmad ibn 'Atiyah.

Sentences of precious matters will pass you – *in sha Allah* the Exalted – as I convey them. He is one of the later [notables] of our country: Damascus, and its surrounding areas: رضي الله عنه.

His lineage is as is stated by Abu Sulaymān.

What we have been narrated to from the Noble Master Abu 'Alī al-Fuḍayl ibn 'Iyāḍ who said: "Those whom we recognise didn't realise what they realised[26] with abundant prayers, or fasting; rather due to a generous soul, sound pure breast[27] and sincerity

25 The study and tracing of lines of descent
26 Meaning they didn't reach the state they attained
27 This denotes a clean heart free from any grudges to others

towards the *Ummah*."
Our Imam al-Shāfi'ī said, "Whomever wants that Allah prescribes goodness for him, then let him have good suspicion in regards to people."
Our Shaykh Imam Abu al-Baqā' informed us, as I read onto him: he said that the Hadith Master Abdul Ghanī informed us (licensing them) that Abu Ṭāhir al-Silafī informed us that Abu Muhammad Abdul Raḥmān ibn Aḥmad al-Dūnī informed us saying: I heard Aba al-Ḥasan 'Alī ibn Muhammad al-Asadabādī say that 'Alī ibn al-Ḥusayn ibn 'Alī informed us that Abu Manṣūr Yaḥyā ibn Aḥmad al-Marwazī said I heard Aba Ṭāhir Muhammad ibn al-Ḥusayn ibn Maymūn saying: I heard Aba Musā Hārūn ibn Musā say: Abu Ḥātim Muhammad ibn 'Idrīs said: I heard Aba Qubaysah say: "I saw Sufyān al-Thawrī in a dream, so I said, 'What has Allah the Exalted done with you?'

He said:

I looked unto my Lord openly so He said to me

'Congratulations for My pleasure on you O Son of Sa'īd

You indeed used to be excessive in standing when the night darkened

Having the tear of a longing one and a determined heart

So, in front of you; choose whichever palace you want

And visit Me, for I am not far from you.'

I said **al-Silafī** is attributed to a grandfather of his, who was nicknamed **Silafa**. This grandfather had a split lip, which in Persian means, the one with three lips. Abu Ṭāhir al-Silafī is one of the Guardian[28] Masters of his time.
Al-Dūnī is attributed to **al-Dūn** which is a village in Khurasān from the province of al-Daynūr.

28 Denotes that he was one who memorised and understood many texts including hadith

Al-Asadabādī is attributed to **Asadabād** a town on a short distance from Hamadhān if you are going to Iraq.

Al-Thawrī is attributed to Banī Thawr ibn 'Abd Manāt ibn 'Udd ibn Ṫābikhah ibn 'Ilyās ibn Muḍar ibn Nizār ibn Ma'ad ibn Adnān.

As for his saying "openly" it means seeing Him without a veil or messenger.

The meaning of "determined" is a truthful loving to Allah. The people of language said the determined is the heart which is shaken by longing love.

Our Shaykh Imam Hadith Master Abu al-Baqā' (may Allah have mercy on him) informed us saying that Abu Muhammad Abdul 'Azīz ibn Ma'ālī informed us that the Judge Abu Bakr al-Khatīb informed us that Abul Fatḥ Muhammad ibn Ahmad ibn Abil Fawāris informed us that Muhammad ibn Ahmad al-Warrāq informed us saying: I heard AbdUllah ibn Sahl al-Rāzī saying: I heard Yahyā ibn Mu'ādh al-Rāzī say: "How many seekers of forgiveness are despised; and [how many] silent ones who are shown mercy. This one says: "I seek forgiveness of Allah" yet his heart is wicked. And the other is silent, yet his heart is in remembrance."

And with the [same] transmission to al-Khatīb who said that Abu al-Ḥasan al-Wā'iẓ narrated to us that he said: I heard Aba AbdUllah ibn 'Atā' al-Rawdhbārī (may Allah have mercy on him) say: "Whoever leaves [his home going] to knowledge wanting to act upon it, then a little amount of knowledge will benefit him."

And with the [same] transmission, Abu AbdUllah ibn 'Atā' said, "Knowledge is suspended pending acting upon it. Actions are suspended due to *ikhlāṣ*. *Ikhlāṣ* for Allah (Exalted be He) inherits understanding from Allah – the Exalted."

I said that what is sought is the beneficial knowledge, as our Imam al-Shāfi'ī said, "Knowledge is not that which is memorised. Rather, knowledge is that which benefits."

Our Shaykh Abu al-Baqā' informed us saying that Abu Muhammad informed us that Abu Bakr informed us that al-Khatīb informed us that 'Alī ibn Maḥmūd al-Ṣufī informed us that Abdul Wahhāb ibn al-Ḥasan al-Kilābī informed us that Sa'id ibn Abdul 'Azīz al-Ḥalabī narrated to them saying: I heard Qāsim al-Jū'ī say: "The foundation of the *dīn* is devoutness.[29] The best of *'ibādah* is the struggle in the night. The best path to *al-Jannah* is a sound pure breast."

The Imam and Hadith master Abu Sa'īd al-Sam'ānī in his book on Genealogy – said that this man Qāsim al-Jū'ī has *karāmāt*. He is attributed to hunger (*Jū'*); and this may be because he used to often remain hungry.

Our Shaykh Abu al-Baqā' informed us saying that Abu Muhammad informed us that Abu Bakr informed us that al-Khatīb informed us that Ahmad ibn al-Ḥusayn ibn al-Sammāk informed us that he said: I heard Aba Bakr al-Duqqī say: I heard Aba Bakr al-Zaqqāq ﷺ say: "This affair of ours is built on four:

1 - We do not eat except from need

2 - We do not sleep except from being overcome

3 - We are not silent except from fear

4 - And we do not speak except for purpose.

As for **al-Duqqī**, then he is of the senior Sufis, and from the people of cognition and *karāmāt*. He passed away in Damascus in Jumada al-'Ūlā in the year 360(AH).

29 The wara' is one of those words that can't be translated without explanation. It is not devoutness only. Rather it is the aspect of one being God conscious and aware of Allah, that you become cautious of not doing the wrong thing, even if this means leaving permissible acts

As for **al-Zaqqāq**: al-Sam'ānī said, "He is attributed to al-Zaqq,[30] working on it and selling it." And he was among the senior Sufis – who had apparent *karāmāt* and evident cognition.

With this same chain to al-Zaqqāq that he said, "Everyone is attributed to a lineage, except the poor: for they are attributed to Allah ﷻ. Every lineage or parentage will be disconnected, except their lineage and parentage; for their lineage is truthfulness and their parentage is poverty."

And we heard from Imam al-Shāfi'ī ؓ in that which was narrated by al-Bayhaqī – may Allah have mercy on him – with his chain from Yūnus ibn AbdUllah; and it was said Ibn Abdul al-'Alā, who said that al-Shāfi'ī ؓ said: "O Aba Musa. If you struggled your utmost in order to please all people, then there is no way to achieving this. So, if this is the case, then make your action and intention sincere for Allah ﷻ."

Our Shaykh Abu al-Baqā' informed us saying that Abu Muhammad informed us that Abu Bakr informed us that al-Khatīb informed us saying that Ahmad ibn al-Ḥusayn al-Wā'iẓ informed us saying: I heard Aba Bakr al-Ṭarsūsī say: I heard Aba Bakr 'Ibrahīm ibn Shaybān saying: I heard Aba AbdUllah al-Maghribī say: "A Sufi without truthfulness: the one who shovels mud is better than him.[31]"

The Story of Ḥammād with Muhammad ibn Sulaymān

We have been narrated to with multiple chains, from Muqātil ibn Ṣālih al-Khurāsānī, who said: I entered onto Ḥammād ibn Salamah ؓ.

30 Al-Zaqq: animal of skin, made into pouches for the carrying of water
31 Referring to the notion that the one who shovels mud has a purpose and he has recognised it, whilst the former is without true purpose

I found there was nothing in the house except a straw mat on which he was sitting, and a *muṣ-ḥaf*[32] he reads from, a folder containing his knowledge and a jug from which he makes *wuḍu*.

So, whilst I was sitting in his presence, someone knocked on the door.

He said: "Oh girl, go out and look who is that!"

She said, "This is the messenger of Muhammad ibn Sulaymān!"

He said: "Tell him that he enters alone."

So he entered, gave salutation and passed him a letter.

He said: "Read it!" So in it was: In the name of Allah, Most Gracious, Most Merciful: From Muhammad ibn Sulaymān to Ḥammād ibn Salamah. As for then, may Allah allow you to enter into the morning with the same with what He has given His *'awliyā'* and the people of His obedience. A question has occurred and we wish to ask you about it.

He said: "Oh girl, come and get me the inkwell!"

Then he said: "Write on the back of this letter: 'Likewise, may Allah allow you to enter into the morning with the same with what He has given His *'awliyā'* and the people of His obedience. We observed the scholars, and they do not come to anyone. If a matter has befallen, then come to us and ask us about what concerns you. If you come to me, do not come to me except by yourself. Do not bring your horsemen and infantry, for then I will not advise you, nor will I advise myself and *salām*!'

So, whilst I was sitting with him, someone knocked on the door.

He said: "Oh girl, go out and look who is it?"

She said: "Muhammad ibn Sulaymān."

He said: "Tell him to enter, alone."

Muhammad ibn Sulaymān entered and greeted, then he sat in front of Ḥammād.

Muhammad said, "Why is it when I look at you, I am filled with terror?!"

32 The term for the Quran Book or papers

Ḥammād said: "I heard Thābit - meaning al-Bunānī - say: I heard Anas ibn Mālik ﷺ say: I heard the Messenger of Allah ﷺ say: **"If the scholar seeks Allah with his knowledge, everything will be in awe of him. Yet, if he seeks to increase his treasures, he will be in awe of everything."**

Muhammad said: "What do you say - may Allah have mercy on you – with regards to a man who has two sons, and he is more pleased with one of them; such that he wants to make two thirds of his money for him while still alive?"

Ḥammād said: "No! And may Allah have mercy on you. For I have heard Thābit al-Bunānī saying: I heard Anas ibn Mālik say: I heard the Messenger of Allah ﷺ say:

"Surely, if Allah ﷻ wants to punish a slave with his [own] money, He will enable him -as he is dying – to write an unfair will."

Muhammad said: "Any need?"

He said: "Give! Unless it is a calamity in the *dīn*!"

Muhammad said: "Forty thousand dirhams[33]! You can use them to seek help in the state you are."

Ḥammād said: "Return it to those whom you have wronged it from!"

He said: "By Allah, I only give you from what I have inherited!"

He said: "I do not need it. Fold it away from me, may Allah fold away your burdens."

He said: "Something else?"

He said: "Give! Unless it is a calamity in the *dīn*!"

He said: "Take it and divide[34] it!"

He said: "It might be that if I am just in its division, some of those who did not get a share, would say that he was not fair in its division, so he would be sinning! Fold it away from me, may Allah fold away your burdens."

33 Traditionally, a dirham is a silver coin. It was used extensively in the past, mentioned in the Quran. Today, a few countries still use the dirham

34 Meaning give it to others

I said: What a great narration this is! What good benefits it contains! And of the treasures which are compiled in it and the alerts to important principles. They are obvious not in need of mentioning.

However, there are some words from the language which need specifying - although they are known – for the purpose of preserving the language.

Muṣ-ḥaf (مصحف) is pronounced as *muṣ-ḥaf* or *miṣ-ḥaf* or *maṣ-ḥaf*. *Muṣ-ḥaf* being the most proper. I have clarified this and shown its derivations in the book "Tahdhīb al-'Asmā' wa al-Lughāt".

[The other Arabic words have not been translated as they would not benefit the non-Arabic speaker.]

Our Shaykh Abu al-Baqā' informed us with my reading on to him saying that Hadith Master Abdul Ghanī informed us – via licence – that Muhammad ibn Abdul Bāqī informed us that Abu al-Ḥasan 'Alī ibn Muhammad al-Khatīb informed them that Abūl Ḥusayn 'Alī ibn Muhammad informed them saying that Abu AbdUllah al-Tamīmī narrated to him from his father who said:
"I saw Ḥammād ibn Salamah in a dream, so I said to him: 'What has Allah done with you?'
He said: "Good!"
I said: "What did He say?"
He said: "He said to me: 'For a long time you tired yourself. Today, I shall elongate your rest, and the rest of those who tire themselves for My sake. *Bakhin Bakhin*[35], what I have prepared for them!'."

35 Words said to display astonishment or delight

09

Chapter of Valuable Words of Wisdom

We have been narrated to in Ṣaḥīḥ al-Bukhārī (may Allah have mercy on him) who said: Ammar [ibn Yāsir] رضي الله عنه said these words:

Three [matters] whoever combines them has attained *īmān*:

1 - Equity of yourself;

2 - Extending *salām* to the world; and

3 - Spending during times of skimpiness.

I said: In these words, he رضي الله عنه has combined the goodness of the Next Life and the *dunyā*. Around these words, Islam orbits. Because whoever is fair to himself in what is Allah's; for the creation of what is on him; and for himself – of advising it, or its maintenance - has reached the goal of obedience.

And his saying: "Extending *salām* to the world", it means to the people, and not being arrogant towards them, i.e. rising above them. It refers to all people, as the Prophet's ﷺ saying:

"And to grant peace to those whom you know and whom you do not know."

This is one of the greatest noble morals. It includes safety from enmities, hatred, and contempt for people and arrogance against them, and rising above them.

As for "spending during times of skimpiness", then it is the climax of generosity!

Allah ﷻ has mentioned praise for this, He said:

﴿وَيُؤْثِرُونَ عَلَىٰ أَنفُسِهِمْ وَلَوْ كَانَ بِهِمْ خَصَاصَةٌ﴾

﴿And they prefer [others] over themselves, even though they have specific needs of their own.﴾[36]

This is general in relation to the man's expenditure on his family, guests, and the person asking him; and every expense in obedience to Allah ﷻ.

And it:

1 - demonstrates dependence on Allah Almighty, and reliance on the breadth of His bounty, and confidence in [His] ensuring livelihood.

2 - also includes asceticism in the world, for not saving its belongings, abandoning interest in it, boasting and multiplying with it.

3 - includes other than what I mentioned of good things, but I have opted in this book for the eloquent abbreviation for fear of boredom.

These words have been narrated to us in "Sharḥ al-Sunnah" by al-Baghawī, on the authority of Ammar ﷺ, on the authority of the Prophet ﷺ, and Allah knows best.

We have been narrated to in Ṣaḥīḥ Muslim (may Allah Almighty have mercy on him) who said that Yaḥyā ibn Yaḥyā narrated to us

36 Holy Quran: Chapter of The Gathering 59:9

saying that AbdUllah ibn Abi Kathīr informed us, that he said: I
heard my father say: "Knowledge is not attainable whilst resting
the body."

We have been narrated to in Ṣaḥīḥ al-Bukhārī 🕮 that he said:
Rabīʿah - meaning the *shaykh* of Mālik ibn Anas the Imam (may
Allah be pleased with them both) said: "It is not befitting for
anyone who has any knowledge, to place himself [down]."

I said: Regarding the meaning of the words of Rabīʿah; there
are two opinions which I have explained both of them in The
Explanation of Ṣaḥīḥ al-Bukhārī and I summarise them here:

1 - One of them: it means whoever has intelligence in knowledge,
    and has acquired some of it; and the signs of eminence have
    appeared in him, he should strive for its development. He
    should not abandon seeking it, as he will lose his attainment
    and he will place himself down.
2 - The second: Its means whoever has gained knowledge, should
    seek to spread it, seeking Allah's pleasure, and he should
    spread it to people to transfer it from him, and people will
    benefit from it, and it benefits him in return.

He should be gentle with whom takes it from him, and should
facilitate the ways of acquiring it, to be more significant in the
sincerity of knowledge; for *dīn* is sincerity.

The companions of al-Shāfiʿī (may Allah have mercy on him)
differed as to the one who was described in the former category:
does he **have to** develop the seeking, and is it prohibited to
abandon? Or does it remain in his right as a communal obligation,
as it was, and he is not forbidden from abandoning it, if someone
else adopts it?

The second opinion above is the view of most of them, and it is the correct chosen one, and Allah knows best.

We have been narrated to on the authority of 'Omar ibn al-Khattāb and his son AbdUllah, may Allah be pleased with them both, that he said: "He whose face has softened, his knowledge will be softened."

Meaning: Whoever is shy to seek knowledge, his knowledge will be thin (soft); that is: little.

We have been narrated to in Ṣaḥīḥ al-Bukhārī ﷺ that Mujāhid - may Allah have mercy on him - said: "He will not learn knowledge: someone who is shy or someone who is arrogant."

We have been narrated to in Ṣaḥīḥ Muslim and others on the authority of 'Ā'ishah (may Allah be pleased with her) that she said: "What great women were the women of al-Anṣār! Shyness did not prevent them from comprehending the *dīn*."

We have been narrated to in Ṣaḥīḥ al-Bukhārī that he said: 'Omar ﷺ said: "Comprehend before you prevail."

Its meaning: Be concerned to master the knowledge, and being able to attain it whilst you are young people with no occupation, no presidency and of no [old] age. For if you become old, and become heads who are followed, you will be denied [the opportunity] of comprehension (learning) and attainment.

This is approximate to what Imam al-Shāfi'ī said: "Understand before you preside. For when you preside, there will be no way for comprehending."

Our Shaykh Abu al-Baqā' informed us saying that Abu Muhammad informed us that Abu Bakr informed us that al-Khatīb informed us saying that Abu Muhammad al-Aṣfahānī told us, that Ja'far al-Khuldī told us that he heard al-Junayd (may Allah Almighty have mercy on him) saying that he heard Sarī say: "I do not wish to die where I am known, for I am afraid that the earth will not accept me, and I will be exposed."

With this same chain of transmission, al-Junayd said:
I heard Sarī saying:
"I look at my nose twice every day, out of fear that my face may have darkened!"

With this transmission to al-Khatīb who said that 'Alī ibn al-Qāsim narrated to us that he said that he heard al-Ḥusayn ibn Arjak say: "Amongst the best talents is the [intellectual] mind, and amongst the worst of calamities is ignorance."

And with this transmission to al-Khatīb who said that Abdul 'Azīz informed us that Muhammad narrated to us that he said that I heard Aba AbdUllah Muhammad ibn AbdUllah - the student of Bishr ibn al-Ḥārith – who said that I heard Ibn al-Ḥārith ﷺ say: "They didn't used to eat out of delicacy, and they didn't used to wear out of luxury."

He said: "This is the way of the hereafter; and that of the Prophets, the righteous, and those who came after them. Whoever claims that the matter is not in this, is deluded!"

With this transmission to al-Khatīb who said: Abdul Raḥmān ibn Muhammad al-Nīsābūrī informed us that Muhammad ibn AbdUllah ibn Bahlūl al-Faqīh narrated to us that Ahmad ibn 'Alī ibn Abi Ḥimyar narrated to us that he said: I heard Sahl ibn AbdUllah – may Allah have mercy on him - saying: "It is forbidden for a heart to smell the aroma of certainty whilst in it there is comfort to other than Allah Almighty! And it is forbidden for a heart to receive the light, whilst it contains something of what Allah Almighty despises."

And with this transmission to al-Khatīb who said that Abu al-Ḥasan Ahmad ibn Muhammad al-Ahwāzī informed us that Abu Abdullah ibn Muhammad ibn Mukhlid al-'Attār narrated to us that Mūsā ibn Hārūn narrated to us that Muhammad - meaning ibn Hayṣam – narrated to us that he said: I heard Bishr – that is the son of al-Ḥārith - may Allah have mercy on him saying: "Allah Almighty revealed to Dāwūd عليه السلام: "O Dāwūd! Do not place between Me and you a deluded scholar; such that he repels you with His delusion from the path to My Love. Surely, they are the highway robbers of My worshipers."

We ask Allah for [His] pardon.

Our [following] three Shaykh Imams informed us:

1 - The Judge Imam, the Remnant[37] of the shaykhs, Abu al-Fadl Abdul Karīm son of the Judge Abi al-Qāsim Abdul Ṣamad ibn Muhammad al-'Anṣārī; and
2 - The Imam Hadith Master Abul Baqā' Khālid ibn Yūsuf; and
3 - The Shaykh Imam Abu AbdUllah Muhammad ibn Abdul Muḥṣin ibn Muhammad ibn Manṣūr al-'Anṣārī,

...the Damascenes, they said: Shaykh Imam Abu al-Yumn Zayd ibn al-Ḥasan al-Kindī informed us that Abu Bakr Muhammad ibn Abdul-Bāqī al-'Anṣārī informed us that Abu 'Isḥāq ibn 'Omar ibn Ahmad al-Barmakī informed us that Abu Muhammad AbdUllah ibn 'Ibrāhīm Nāshi' informed us that Abu Muslim ibn Abdullah al-Kaḥḥī informed us that Muhammad ibn AbdUllah al-'Anṣārī narrated to us that Sulaymān al-Taymī narrated to us on the

37 This description is an intense praise, saying that this shaykh is one of the remaining people holding great knowledge authority of Abu ʿOthmān al-Nahdī on the authority of Salmān ﷺ who said: "If people knew Allah's help for the weak, they would not have overpriced the carriage.[38]"

Al-Shāfiʿī ﷺ said: "You should practice abstinence! Ascetism on an ascetic is better than jewellery on a young woman.[39]"

Al-Rabīʿ (may Allah have mercy on him) said: Al-Shāfiʿī ﷺ said to me: "O Rabīʿ! Do not speak about that which does not concern you. For when you speak the word, it owns you and you do not own it." Al-Muzanī (may Allah have mercy on him) said: I heard al-Shāfiʿī ﷺ say: "There isn't anyone who doesn't have someone who loves him and someone who hates him. So, if there is no other option, let one be with the people of obedience to Allah ﷻ."

We have been narrated to from the authority of al-Ḥasan ibn ʿImrān ibn ʿUyaynah that Sufyān ibn ʿUyaynah told him in Muzdalifah in the last Hajj he performed: "I have fulfilled coming to this place seventy times. Each time I say, 'O Allah! Do not make it the last time in relation to this place!' However, I am embarrassed from Allah ﷻ from the numerous times that I have asked Him."
So, he returned [home] and he passed away the following year.

Shaykh al-Amīn al-Sayyid Abu al-Fadl Muhammad ibn Muhammad ibn Muhammad ibn al-Taymī al-Bakrī informed us, with my reading on him that I read at the Kallāsah[40] of the Damascus Mosque - that he said Shaykh Abu Ḥafṣ ʿOmar ibn Muhammad ibn Muʿammar ibn Ṭibrzad informed us that he said that Hadith Master Abu al-Qāsim Ismāʿīl ibn Ahmad ibn ʿOmar al-Samarqandī informed us that he said: I heard Abdul Dāʾim

38 A profound statement which can carry many meanings, amongst of which is that overpricing the carriage means that they search for the material gains, when material is no relevance to the station one has with Allah

39 The precise translation of nāhid is a "full breasted woman" which is a symbol of beauty. Allah mentions this as well as a description of the women in al-Jannah. See the Chapter of the News 78:33

40 The name of the Northern Gate, under the minaret, named like that which is derived from limescale, as it overlooked the section of the city in which they worked on limestone

ibn al-Ḥasan al-Hilālī say: I heard Abdul Wahhāb ibn al-Ḥasan al-Kilābī say: I heard Muhammad ibn Khuraym al-'Uqaylī say: I heard Ahmad ibn Abi al-Hawārī say: I wished to see Abu Sulaymān al-Dārānī - may Allah have mercy on him - in a dream. Indeed, I saw him after one year.

I said to him: "Teacher! What has Allah done to you?"

He said: "O Ahmad! I came out from the small gate, and I found a sack of barley, so I took a stick from it. I can't remember [what I did with it]: I cleaned in between my teeth with it or I threw it. Because of it, I am being accounted for a whole year till this night."

I said: What a great story this is, in urging piety and warning against leniency in belittled[41] grievances!

Our Shaykh, the righteous Imam, the precise Hadith Master Abu 'Isḥāq 'Ibrāhīm ibn 'Isā ibn Yūsuf al-Murādī informed me with my reading on him that Shaykh Imam Abu al-Ḥasan ibn HibatUllah al-Ḥimyarī informed us that the Hadith Master Abu Ṫāhir al-Silafī informed us that Imam Abu Bakr Ahmad ibn Muhammad ibn Zinjawayh al-Zinjawī informed us that Abu Ṫālib Yaḥyā ibn 'Alī al-Daskarī said: I heard Abu Ahmad al-Ghatrīfī say: I heard Aba al-'Abbās Muhammad ibn 'Isḥāq al-Sarrāj say: I heard AbdUllah ibn Muhammad al-Warrāq say: They passed by Ma'rūf during the days of strife going to fight; and he would say to them: "Pass by, may Allah accompany you! Pass by, May Allah bless you!"

He was told that they are going out to fight!

He said: "If Allah accompanies them, they will not fight."

41 Which in reality that are not little at all

10

Good fragments of Advice from those who know

Our Shaykh Abu 'Isḥāq informed us with this transmission to al-Sarrāj, who said: I heard Ibn Abi al-Dunyā say that some people sat down in the presence of Ma'ruf , and one of them back-bit another man. So he [Ma'ruf] said to him: "Oh So-and-so! Remember the day when cotton will be placed on your eyes.[42]"

And with this chain of transmission, al-Sarrāj said: I heard Yaḥyā ibn Abī Tālib say: I heard Ya'qūb ibn Ma'rūf say: I heard my uncle say: "Speech in matters which do not concern one, is a let-down from Allah Almighty."

With this chain of transmission, al-Sarrāj said: I heard 'Alī ibn al-Muwaffaq say: 'The following was Ma'rūf's supplication:

يَا مَالِكُ، يَا قَدِير، يَا مَن لَيسَ لَهُ نَظِير

"O Supreme Owner! O Able! O You who has no counterpart"!'

With this attribution to al-Ghatrīfī who said that Abu al-Ḥasan al-Tājir informed us and he said that Salamah ibn Shabīb narrated to us that Khalaf ibn Tamīm narrated to us that he said:

42 Reference to death, as you will be washed on the table

I saw Ibn 'Ad-ham in al-Shām[43], so I asked him: "What has brought you here?"
He said: "As for me, I did not come here for *jihād* nor for army stationing, but I came so I can eat my fill of halal bread."

We have been narrated to on the authority of Hadith Master Ahmad ibn AbdUllah al-'Ijlī who said: Rab'ī ibn Ḥirāsh was a trustworthy follower, never lying. He had two sons who were rebellious[44] during the time of al-Ḥajjāj.
It was said to al-Ḥajjāj: "Their father has never lied, if you send for him and asked him about them?"
He sent for him and was asked: "Where are your sons?"
He said: "They are at home!"
Al-Ḥajjāj said: "We have pardoned them because of your honesty!"

Al-Ḥārith al-Ghazzī said that Rabī' Ibn Ḥirāsh swore an oath that he would not laugh, until he knew where his fate was. So, he only laughed after his death!
And his brother, Rab'ī - after him – [also] swore an oath that he would not laugh until he knows whether he is in *al-Jannah* or in the Fire!
Al-Ḥārith said: His washer[45] told me that he continued to smile on his bed, whilst we were washing him until we finished!

We have been narrated to on the authority of Ahmad ibn AbdUllah, who said: The [Quran] reciters of the people of Kūfah met in the home of al-Hakam ibn 'Otaybah. They unanimously agreed that the most prominent reciter of the people of Kūfah was Ṫalhah ibn Muṣarrif.
So when he [Ṫalhah] heard of this, he went to sit [as a student] with al-'A'mash and recite onto him, in order that this title would no longer be attributed to him!

43 Translated as the Levant, it includes present day Syria, Jordan, Palestine and Lebanon
44 Meaning armed resistance
45 Meaning the one who washes the dead person

On the authority of Imam al-Shāfi'ī (may Allah have mercy on him) who said: It was said to 'Ubay Ibn Ka'ab: "O Aba Mundhir! Advise me."
He said: "Befriend your brothers in accordance with their piety. And do not make your tongue an initiator for those who do not want it. And do not envy the living except how you envy the dead."

On the authority of al-Shāfi'ī (may Allah Almighty have mercy on him) who said that Fuḍayl ibn 'Iyāḍ said: "How many a person circumambulates[46] this House; whilst another is distant from it yet rewarded greater than him [the former]."

On the authority of al-Shāfi'ī who narrates from the authority of Fuḍayl who said: "Dāwūd the Prophet said: 'My God! Be for my son Sulaymān after me as you have been for me!'
So, Allah Almighty revealed to him: 'O Dāwūd, tell your son Sulaymān to be to Me as you were to Me, I will be to him as I was to you'."

On the authority of al-Shāfi'ī ﷺ who said: Hishām ibn Abdul Malik said to al-Fuḍayl: "Raise your need to me!"[47]
He said: "I have raised it to the Most Munificent, Most Generous."

And we have been narrated to in the Message of 'Ustādh Abu al-Qāsim al-Qushayrī (may Allah have mercy on him) in the section of the *karāmāt* of the *'awliyā'* of Allah, who said, "Ja'far al-Khuldī had a ring with a gem. One day, he lost it in the Tigris river[48]. He had a tried-and-tested *du'ā'* for returning lost property. So, he made that *du'ā'*, and he found his ring amongst some of his papers that he was looking through.

46 To do ṭawāf
47 Denoting a form of application for support
48 In Iraq

Al-Qushayrī continues: "I heard Aba Ḥātim al-Sijistānī say: 'I heard Aba Nasr al-Sarrāj say that this *du'ā'* is:

يَا جَامِعَ النَّاسِ لِيَومٍ لا رَيبَ فِيه، اجمَع بَينِي وَبَينَ ضَالَّتِي

"O You who gathers people to a Day that will undoubtedly occur, gather me with my lost [item]."

Imam al-Nawawī said: I have tried this *du'ā'* and I have found it beneficial mostly when trying to find a lost item – quickly; and it hasn't failed.
And I heard my Shaykh Abu al-Baqā' say something similar and he is the one who taught it to me.

As for Ja'far al-Khuldī: The Hadith Master and Imam Abu Sa'īd al-Sam'ānī said in his book of Genealogy:

Al-Khuld: A locality in Baghdad, to which is attributed Ṣubayḥ ibn Sa'īd, the narrator from 'Othmān ibn 'Affān and 'Aishah, may Allah be pleased with them.

As for Ja'far ibn Muhammad ibn Naṣr al-Khuldī al-Khawwās, Abu Muhammad is one of the senior Sufis, with apparent *karāmāt*. He was renowned for his name: "al-Khuldī" because one day, he was with al-Junayd.
Al-Junayd was asked about an issue, so he said to Ja'far: "Answer them!"
So, he answered them.
Al-Junayd said to him: "Where did you get these answers from?"
He said: "From my *khuld* [which means mind / heart]"
So, this name [Khuldī] stuck to him.
He died in the year 348AH. Al-Dāraquṭnī narrated from him; as did Abu Ḥafṣ ibn Shāhīn, and others, and he was trustworthy. He narrated from al-Ḥārith ibn Abi 'Usāmah and others.

Ahmad ibn Abi al-Ḥawārī said in the Book of al-Zuhd: I heard
some of our companions, I think it was Abu Sulaymān – referring
to al-Dārānī - ◈ who said: "Iblīs has a devil named "Mutaqāḍ":
he pursues up the son of Adam for [up to] twenty years trying to
make him expose his secret actions to bring them about in public,
so that he loses the reward difference between doing it in secret
and in public."

We have been narrated to from the authority of 'Ibrāhīm ibn Sa'īd
who said: I said to Abu Sa'ad ibn 'Ibrāhīm: "With what did al-
Zuhrī surpass you?
He said: "He would come to the gatherings from their front, and
not from the rear. And there would not remain in the gathering
a young man except he would question him; nor a middle-aged[49]
man except he would question him; nor a boy except he would
question him; nor an old woman except he would question her.
Then he would approach a house from the houses of al-Anṣār, and
he would not leave a young man except he would question him;
nor a middle-aged man except he would question him; nor an old
woman except he would question her; nor a middle-aged woman
except he would question her. He would even try with those who
wear anklets.[50]"

One of the best disciplines with which one can use to discipline
oneself in abandoning care of the sense of clothing, food and
drink, and the like; is what we have been narrated to from the
Commander of the Faithful 'Omar Ibn al-Khattāb ◈ with our
chain of transmission to Abu 'Awānah al-'Isfarāyīnī who said:
Abu Ḥabīb al-Miṣṣīṣī narrated to us that Ḥajjāj narrated to us that
he said: I heard Shu'bah narrate from Qatādah who said: I heard
Abu 'Othmān al-Nahdī (may Allah Exalted have mercy on him)
who said: "While we were in Azerbaijan with 'Utabah ibn Farqad,
we received a letter from 'Omar ibn al-Khattāb [which read]:

---

49 Middle-aged is the one who has passed the age of youth, but not reached old age. Usually between 30 and 50
50 Referring to young women

As for then:
Wear the *'Izār*[51], the *rīdā'*[52] and sandals; and throw away the *khuffs*[53].
Abandon the pants (trousers); and dress with the dress of your father Ismā'īl ﷺ.
Beware of [indulging in] luxuries, and beware of wearing the clothes of the non-Arabs.[54]
I advise you with the sun: for it is the bath of the Arabs.
Wear the clothes of your father: Ma'ad.
Roughen up, and balance [your stature].
Cut up the [horses'] stirrups.[55]
Throw the arrows, and mount the horses by leaping [on their backs]."

Abu 'Othmān al-Nahdī is attributed to one of his grandfathers, whose name is "Nahd ibn Zaid ibn Layth". The name of Abu 'Othmān is Abdul Raḥmān ibn Mall, or Mull, or Mill, or it is Mil'.

He [Abu 'Othmān] is one of the senior Followers, and is considered *mukhaḍḍram*[56] who is defined as someone who was alive during the era of ignorance (pre Islam), Islam and the life of the Messenger of Allah ﷺ, yet did not see him ﷺ.
I have showed this amount of his state in the [book] 'Irshād in the hadith sciences, which I have summarised from the book of Shaykh Abu 'Amr ibn al-Ṣalāḥ (may Allah Almighty have mercy on him).
Abu 'Othmān (may Allah have mercy on him) was someone of great importance and high status. He said: "I reached about one hundred and thirty years, and there is nothing which I have not denied[57] except my hope, for I find it as it is."
When al-Ḥusayn ؓ was killed, Abu 'Othmān moved from al-

51 Wraparound, worn on the lower part of the body
52 The Upper cloak for the upper part of the body
53 Khuff is like a leather sock or shoe
54 In this context, refers to the Persians
55 Part of the saddle in which the rider's feet are placed; provides support and leverage to the rider
56 Mukhaḍḍram: someone who has lived through several epochs
57 Meaning it has altered

Kūfah[58] to al-Baṣrah; and said: "I am not going to reside in a country where the son of the Messenger of Allah ﷺ was killed!" He died in the year 95 AH; others have said in the year 100AH. May Allah the Exalted have mercy on him.

And his saying: Azerbaijan, is a well-known region. Pronounced [in Arabic] as Adhrabījān or Ādharbījān.

And his saying: "Wear the clothes of your father Ma'ad" means adorn in the habit of your father, Ma'ad ibn 'Adnān, in the roughness of life.

And his saying: "mount the horses by leaping" means: when you ride a horse, mount it from the ground and do not use a ramp or the like. And do not mount the horses using the stirrups used by the Persians in their saddles.

The story of Jābir and Shihāb ﵄

The Shaykh and Jurist al-Musnid[59] Abu Muhammad Abdul Raḥmān ibn Sālim ibn Yaḥyā al-'Anbārī informed us that he said: Hadith Master Abdul Qādir al-Rahāwī informed us that he said: Judge Abu Sulaymān Dāwūd ibn Muhammad ibn al-Ḥusayn al-Khālidī narrated to us that he said: 'Omar ibn Muhammad ibn Ahmad al-Dimashqī narrated to us that he said: Al-Ḥasan ibn Abdul Malik informed us that al-Ḥusayn ibn Muhammad ibn Nu'aym informed us that AbdUllah ibn Ahmad ibn Ya'qūb informed us that al-Ḥasan ibn Sufyān informed us that Muhammad ibn Marzūq narrated to us that Muslim ibn 'Ibrāhīm narrated to us that 'Isā ibn Ḥumayd al-Rāsī Abu Hammam narrated to us that Abu Hafs al-Naḍr narrated to us from the authority of Jābir ibn AbdUllah al-'Anṣārī, may Allah be pleased with them – that a man came asking him about the

58 Two cities in Iraq, engaged in some rivalry mainly in the Arabic Language
59 Someone who transmits hadith with its full chain of transmission

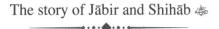

veiling of the believer.

I [Jābir] said, "I am not that person. Rather that is a man called: Shihāb."

So, Jābir walked with him to go to the Governor[60] of that town- a man named: Maslamah. He approached the door, and said to the guard: "Tell the Ruler to come down to me!"

The guard entered whilst smiling, and the Governor said to him: "What's the matter with you?"

He said: "There's a man at the door on a camel and he said: 'Tell the Ruler to come down to me!'."

He said: "Didn't you ask him who he is?!"

So, the guard returned to him and asked him. He said, "I am Jābir ibn AbdUllah al-'Anṣārī."

The guard returned and informed the Governor, who sprung from his seat, and leaned out [of the window]: "Come up!"

Jābir said: "I don't want to come up; but tell me where is Shihāb's home?"

He said: "Come up, and I will send for him to come and fulfil your need."

He said: "I do not want your messenger to go to him; for if the Messenger of the Ruler came to a man it may alarm him. And I would hate for a Muslim man to be startled because of me."

So, the Governor came down, joined Jābir and walked with him until he came to Shihāb. So, Shihāb leaned out and said: "Either you come up or I come down to you?"

Jābir said: "I don't want you to come down to us, and we don't want to go up to you! But narrate to us the hadith that you heard from the Messenger of Allah ﷺ regarding the veiling of a believer."

He said: I heard the Prophet ﷺ say:

"Whoever veils his believing brother; then it is as if he has given him life."

60 Meaning the governor of the town

11

Honouring those because of their relation to the beloved

What they sang in honouring those who have connection to the beloved is the saying of one of them (as prose):

Alas, salute the dwellings in Su'd for truly
I love those dwellings for Fātimah loves them

(Su'd) is a name of a town in the region of Nakhl [the capital of the Old Sinai region].

Abu Bakr al-Hamdānī said in the book of Ishtiqāq: Its origin is Su'd the plural of Sa'īd.

This [poetry] is similar to another's saying:

I love the spinster women as Buthaynah is a spinster
As I love those who are married, when you will get married

This line of poetry is a form of novel writings, as it changes from the third person to the second person. As he said (Buthaynah) then he said: (you will get married).

It has equivalents in the Holy Quran, as in the Almighty's saying:

﴿عَبَسَ وَتَوَلَّى، أَن جَاءَهُ الأَعمَى، وَمَا يُدرِيكَ لَعَلَّهُ يَزَّكَّى﴾

﴿He frowned and turned away. That the blind one had come to him. And what do you know that he may be purified…﴾[61]

And Allah Almighty said:

﴿الحَمدُ اللهِ رَبِّ العَالَمِينَ﴾

﴿Praise be to Allah, Lord of the worlds﴾[62]

until He said:

﴿إِيَّاكَ نَعبُدُ﴾

﴿It is You, we worship﴾[63]

Its reversal, which is the return from the second person to the third person, is demonstrated in what the Almighty said:

﴿حَتَّى إِذَا كُنتُم فِي الفُلكِ وَجَرَينَ بِهِم﴾

﴿…till when you were in the ark, and we ran them into...﴾[64]

61 Holy Quran: He Frowned 80:1-3
62 Holy Quran: The Opening 1:2
63 Holy Quran: The Opening 1:5
64 Holy Quran: Yūnus 10:22

12

Consequences of Mockery

Al-'Anbārī informed us that Abdul Hāfiẓ informed us that Abdul Qādir al-Rahāwī informed us that Abdul Raḥīm ibn 'Alī al-Shāhid informed us that Muhammad ibn Ṫāhir al-Maqdisī al-Hāfiẓ informed us that Abu al-Fatḥ al-Muqqayid informed us that Abu al-Ḥasan ibn 'Alī ibn Muhammad ibn Ṫalḥah informed us that Sulaymān ibn Ahmad ibn Ayūb al-Ṫabarānī narrated to us that he said: I heard Aba Yaḥyā Zakariya ibn Yaḥyā al-Sājī - may Allah have mercy on him - say: "We were walking in the alleys of al-Baṣrah to the door of some of the [Hadith] narrators, so I hurried in my walk. A heretic in his religion was accompanying a man among them. The heretic said mockingly: 'Lift your feet from the wings of the angels, so you do not break them!' After saying this, he became fixated in his place, his legs having dried up and he fell!"

The Hadith Master Abdul Hāfiẓ said: The chain of transmission of this story is as if one were to find it, or like seeing it with one's own eyes, because its narrators are renowned imams.

With the [same] transmission to al-Maqdisī who said: Abu al-Ḥasan Yaḥyā ibn al-Ḥusayn al-Alwi informed us that Abu al-Ḥusayn al-Ḍab'ī informed that he said: I heard AbdUllah ibn Muhammad al-'Akbarī say: I heard Abu AbdUllah Muhammad ibn Ya'qūb al-Mattūthī say: I heard Aba Dāwūd al-Sijistānī say: "There was a man who was amongst the people of hadith: he was a rogue. He heard the hadith of the Prophet ﷺ:

"The angels lower their wings for the seeker of knowledge, contented with what he does".

This man put iron nails in the heels [of his sandals] saying: 'I want to step on the wings of the angels!'

So, he was afflicted with gangrene in his legs."

Imam Abu AbdUllah Muhammad ibn Ismā'īl ibn Muhammad ibn al-Faḍl al-Taymī (may Allah have mercy on him) stated in his book explaining Ṣaḥīḥ Muslim, this story. There, it reads: "His legs were paralyzed, as were his arms and all his limbs."

He said: In some accounts, I saw that it read "...and his physique deteriorated!"

He said: In some stories, I read that one of the innovators had heard the saying of the Prophet ﷺ:

"When one of you wakes up from his sleep, let him not dip his hand in the container until he has washed it, for he does not know where his hand has remained overnight."

The innovator said, as a matter of cynicism: "I know where my hand has remained overnight: in bed!" So, he awoke with his hand in his anus, all the way up to his forearm!

Al-Taymī said: "Let one beware with regards to degrading the *Sunan*[65] and matters of fixed legislation. See how the despicable nature of their actions ended."

65 Plural of sunnah; and refers to the acts of the Prophet ﷺ

I said: The meaning of this hadith, as what Imam al-Shāfi'ī and other scholars ﷺ have said: That the sleeping person's hand floats over his body during his sleep; so he cannot guarantee that it does not pass over an impurity such as blood from a pimple, or a lice or insect; or the place of *istinjā'*[66], and the like. And Allah knows best.

I said: Another narration which falls into the same category is what was observed in our time and the news was multiply transmitted and confirmed with the judges: that a man in the village of Bosra[67], in the early years of 665AH, had a bad opinion and suspicion in the people of goodness. He had a son who believed in them.

One day, his son returned from a righteous shaykh and with him was a *siwāk*.[68]

He said - mockingly: "What's that your shaykh has given you?"

He said: "This toothbrush."

So, the father took it from him and put it in his anus as a sign of contempt for him!

A period passed by, then the man who inserted the toothbrush in his anus, egested a small pup from his anus, closely resembling a fish. So, the man killed it. Then he died immediately, or two days later.

May Allah Almighty relieve us of His calamities, and may He guide us to honour the *Sunan* and to venerate His sacrements!

66 Refers to one's frontal and rear passages
67 Not to be confused with Baṣrah, the latter being a city in Iraq, and the former a city in present day Syria
68 Toothbrush

13

Further Words of Guidance

The Shaykh and guided Jurist Abu Muhammad Abdul Raḥmān ibn Sālim al-'Anbārī (may Allah have mercy on) informed us that the Judge and Imam Abu al-Qāsim Abdul Ṣamad ibn Muhammad ibn Abi al-Faḍl al-'Anṣārī informed us that Imam Abu al-Fatḥ Naṣr Ullah ibn Muhammad ibn Abdul Qawī al-Miṣīṣī informed us that the Shaykh and Faqīh Abu al-Fatḥ Naṣr ibn 'Ibrāhīm al-Maqdisī al-Zāhid ﵁ informed us that the Judge Abu al-Ḥasan Muhammad ibn 'Alī informed us, as he wrote to me, he said that Ahmad ibn Ya'qūb al-Herawī informed us that Abu AbdUllah al-Rūzbādī narrated to us that 'Omar ibn Mukhalad al-Ṣufī narrated to us that he said: **Ibn Abī al-Ward said: Ma'rūf al-Karkhī said: "The mark of Allah Almighty's despise for a slave is that you see him occupied with what does not concern him."**

Our Shaykh Hadith Master Abu al-Baqā' (may Allah have mercy on him) informed us that Abu Muhammad informed us that the Judge Abū Bakr informed us that al-Khatīb Abu Bakr informed us that Abu Sa'īd - meaning Muhammad ibn Mūsā ibn al-Faḍl ibn 'Ibrāhīm – informed us that he said: **I heard al-Fuḍayl ibn 'Iyāḍ - may Allah Almighty have mercy on him - say: "You ask Paradise of Him, yet you do what He despises. I have not seen anyone having a lower opinion of himself than you."**

Abu al-Baqā' informed us that Abu Muhammad narrated to us that Abu Bakr al-Khatīb narrated to us that Abu al-Qāsim Abdul Raḥmān ibn al-Sarrāj informed us that he said: I heard Abu Bakr Ahmad ibn Muhammad al-Sāyiḥ that he said: I heard al-Qāsim ibn Muhammad – the companion of Sahl - saying: I heard Sahl ibn AbdUllah say:"There is no thicker veil between the slave and Allah than a [false] claim! And there is no closer path to Him than impoverishment."

We have been narrated to with authentic chains on the authority of Abu Yaḥyā al-Bakrāwī who said: "I did not see anyone more worshiping of Allah than Shu'bah,[69] to the extent his skin dried off his bone, as there was no flesh between them."

We have been conveyed to from al-Shāfi'ī (may Allah have mercy on him) who said:
The best of the *dunyā* and the hereafter is in five characteristics:
1 - Enrichment of the Self.
2 - Avoiding Harm.
3 - Earning halal.
4 - The dress of piety; and
5 - Trust in Allah ﷻ in all states.

On the authority of al-Shāfi'ī ﷺ he said: "He who is overwhelmed by the intensity of lust for the *dunyā*, shall be enslaved to its people. And he who is happy with subservience [to Allah], subjugation [to others] will be dispelled away from him."

Al-Shāfi'ī ﷺ said: "Whoever loves for Allah to open his heart and to give him knowledge, then he must practise solitude, reduce his food intake; and abandon socialising with fools as well as some of those associated with knowledge who have no fairness or morals."

69 Shu 'bah ibn al-Ḥajjāj (d. 160AH) The famous Imam and Hadith Master

Al-Shāfi'ī ﷺ said: "The most beneficial of munitions is piety; and the most harmful of it is aggression."
Al-Shāfi'ī ﷺ said: The best actions are three:

1 - The remembrance of Allah Almighty.

2 - Consoling brothers.

3 - Being fair to people.

It means these three are of the best works.

Al-Shāfi'ī (may Allah Almighty have mercy on him) said: "Hypocrisy is not known except by a sincere one."

Meaning that one cannot know its reality and see its hidden aspects, except he who seeks sincerity. He strives for a long time searching, thinking and excavating for it, until he knows it or some of it; and all this does not occur to anyone; rather, this happens to the select.

As for an ordinary person who claims that he knows hypocrisy, then he is ignorant of its reality. And I will mention in this book a chapter – *in sha Allah* Almighty - you will see in it of the wonders which will bring satisfaction to your eyes, *in sha Allah*.

It is sufficient for its[70] intense concealment what we have narrated from 'Ustadh Imam Abu al-Qāsim al-Qushayrī (may Allah have mercy on him) in his "Al-Risālah"[71] with his aforementioned chain.

He said: I heard Muhammad ibn al-Ḥusayn say: I heard Ahmad ibn 'Alī ibn Ja'far say: I heard al-Ḥasan ibn 'Alawiyyah say: Abu Yazīd[72] ﷺ said: "For twelve years I was the blacksmith of my soul. For five years I was the mirror of my heart. And for one year I was observing in between the two. [I realised] In my middle was an apparent girdle; so I worked for twelve years to cut it, thinking

70 Referring to sincerity
71 The Letter: an important treatise of 'Ustādh al-Qushayrī in Sufism
72 Abu Yazīd al-Bisṭāmī (d. 261AH)

how to remove it. [And I realised] I had an internal girdle; so I worked for five years to cut it, thinking of how to remove it. It was then made apparent to me, and I looked at the creation, and I saw them dead. So, I pronounced on them four *takbīrs*[73]!"

I said: It is sufficient for the intense concealment of showing-off, that it is confusing even for this master, who is unique in this path. With regard to his saying: "I saw them dead", then it is a highly precious and well-informed statement; very rare to find words like it in the words of someone who is not the Prophet ﷺ which give the same meaning.

I refer to its explanation in a brief statement: Its meaning is that when he struggled this struggle, and his self was refined, his heart enlightened; and he conquered his self and subdued it, and owned it with full possession; and it followed him absolutely. After all this happened, he looked at all the creatures and found them dead without any effect. They do not harm nor benefit. Nor do they give or prevent. They do not give life nor take it away. They do not connect nor cut off; nor do they bring things close or distance them. They do not make others happy or sad; and they do not provide [for others] nor restrict. They do not own for themselves benefit or harm; nor do they own death, life, or resurrection. This is the attribute of the dead; so they should be treated as dead in these aforementioned matters.

They should not be feared nor anticipated; and one should not seek what is in their possession. Their attention should not be sought, nor should they be softened towards, nor should one occupy himself with them, nor should they be viewed with contempt, nor should they be despised. Their faults should not be mentioned, their blunders shouldn't be pursued, their trips shouldn't be searched for. They should not be envied, and one should not consider what Allah has given them of gifts as much. Mercy should be invoked for them, and they should be excused for what they bring of shortcomings…although we will still

73 Indicative of the funeral prayer

establish the prescribed punishments on them.
The establishment of punishments should not prevent us from the endeavour to veil their faults and to avoid belittling them, as one does with the deceased. And if someone makes ill mention of them, we forbid them from doing so as we would do so if he mentioned the dead with something bad.
Also, we do not do anything for them[74], nor do we abstain from doing anything for their sake. We do not cease any act of Allah's obedience because of them; just as we do not stop that because of the dead.
We do not care about their praise [for us] and we are not fond of it, nor do we hate their abuse towards us, and we do not reciprocate.
The conclusion is that they are like nothing in all of what we have mentioned, because they are subdued and ruled by the laws of Allah Almighty. Therefore, whoever treats them in this way, would have combined the good of the Hereafter and the *dunyā*.
We ask Allah the Most Generous, to grant us success to this.
These words are sufficient to indicate the explanation of his words ﷺ, and Allah knows best.

We have been narrated to with our chain to al-Qushayrī (may Allah Almighty have mercy on him) that he said: I heard Shaykh Abu Abdul Raḥmān al-Sulamī, the Imam of Sufism in his time and later times that he said: I heard al-'Abbās al-Baghdādī say: I heard Ja'far say: I heard al-Junayd say: I heard al-Sarī say:
"O Youth! Be serious in your efforts before you reach my stage; then you will weaken and fall short as I have fallen short."
He said: "At the time of his statement, even the youth could not catch up with him in his worship!"

Ahmad ibn Abi al-Ḥawārī said in "Kitāb al-Zuhd": Suwayd narrated to us that he said: I saw Ibn Abi Mirthad in the market; in

74 Meaning we do not actions seeking their approval. It does not mean that we do not do actions which benefit them, like du'ā' and charity

his hand was some bread and a bone with little meat on it, and he was eating of it. Prior to his, he was called for the Judiciary; and he did so until he escaped [being appointed as a judge][75].

What is similar to this is what Imam al-Bayhaqī narrated with his chain of transmission from the authority of Imam al-Shāfiʿī (may Allah Almighty have mercy on him) that he said: "Sufyān al-Thawrī ☙ entered on to the Commander of the Faithful[76], making himself appear insane. He would stroke the rug and say: 'How excellent is this! What did you pay for it?'

And he would say, 'Urine! Urine!'

Until he was expelled; meaning that he fooled them to get away from the Ruler and be free from their affairs.

Al-Shāfiʿī ☙ said: The son of al-Ḥusayn ibn ʿAlī - may Allah Almighty be pleased with them both - died, and so misery was not noticed on him!

He was reproached for this. So, he said: "We are the Ahl ul-Bayt:[77] we ask Allah the Exalted, and He grants us. So, if He wants something which we dislike, yet He wishes, we are content."

Ahmad ibn Abi al-Ḥawārī said: I heard Abu Sulaymān say: "We do not love those we love except for their obedience to their tutors. Yet you disobey me, I have commanded you to extend your fingers[78]."
In the narration of al-Tirmidhī [it reads]: "to grasp".

On the authority of Saʿīd ibn Jubayr ☙ who looked towards his son and said: "I know a quality in you!"
He said: "What is it?"
He said, "You will die! And I will anticipate[79] this."

---

75 Eating in the markets was considered poor manners, and especially for those who had raised status. Doing this openly would be a stain on one's character
76 The Caliph
77 People of the Household of the Prophet ﷺ ; those who come from his lineage ﷺ or close proximity
78 Meaning in salah, during tashahhud
79 Meaning he will anticipate the reward for being patient on the loss of a loved one

On the authority of Abu al-Ḥasan al-Madā'īnī who said: "It was said to a Bedouin woman: 'How good is your grief on your son!' She said: 'The loss of his father has made me forget all misfortunes after that'."

Mūsā ibn al-Muhtadī told 'Ibrāhīm ibn Muslim, as he comforted him with the loss of his son. He said: "[He is] Your happiness: yet he is a trial and tribulation. [He is] Your sadness: which are prayers and mercy."

He said: A man wrote to one of his brothers comforting him with the loss of his son:"As for then; the child for his parent is sorrow and strife for as long as he is alive; and if he precedes him, he is prayer and mercy. So, do not despair on what you have missed of his sorrow and his tribulation; and do not lose what Allah Almighty has compensated you of his prayers and mercy."

Ahmad ibn Abi al-Ḥawārī said: I heard Abu Sulaymān say: "I remained twenty years not having a wet dream. I enacted in Makkah an act; so I woke up having had a wet dream[80]."

I said to him, "What was the act?"

He said: "I left the 'Ishā' prayer in the Sacred Mosque in congregation."

We have been narrated to from the authority of Imam Mālik ﷺ: "You would meet a man and he doesn't stutter; not even a letter. However, his actions are all stutters."

We have been narrated to on the authority of Imam Abu Bakr Muhammad ibn Yaḥyā ibn AbdUllah ibn 'Abbās ibn Muhammad ibn Ṣawl al-Maṣūlī: Some of the ascetics said:"We expressed in our speech such we did not stutter. [Yet] we faltered in our actions such that we did not express ourselves!"

80 They used to consider having wet dreams as a defect, even though it is out of one's control

The poet said:

We were not flawed from ignorance, but
we conceal knowledge with ignorance
We hate to falter in our speech
yet we do not care about stuttering in our actions

Our Shaykh Abu Muhammad Ismāʻīl ibn Abi Isḥāq informed us from 'Ibrāhīm ibn Abi al-Bishr Shākir that he informed us that Abu Ṫāhir Barakāt ibn 'Ibrāhīm ibn Ṫāhir al-Khushūʻī informed us that Abu Muhammad Hibat Ullah ibn Ahmad ibn Muhammad al-Akfānī informed us that Abu Bakr Ahmad ibn ʻAlī ibn Thābit al-Baghdādī al-Ḥafiẓ narrated to us that ʻUbayd Ullah ibn ʻOmar al-Wāʻiẓ informed us saying that my father narrated to me that Muhammad ibn Naṣr ibn ʻAlī al-Jahḍamī narrated to us that Muhammad ibn Khālid narrated to me that ʻAlī ibn Naṣr narrated to us that he said: I saw al-Khalīl ibn Ahmad - may Allah the Almighty have mercy on him - in a dream. So, I said in my dream: 'I do not see anyone more intellectual than al-Khalīl!' So I said: 'What has Allah done with you ?'
He said: "Did you see where we were? For there was nothing better than Subḥān Allah, al-Ḥamdu Lillāh, Lā 'ilāha illā Allah and Allahu Akbar[81]."

In another narration: ʻAlī ibn Naṣr said: I saw al-Khalīl ibn Ahmad in a dream, so I said to him: "What did your Lord do with you?"
He said: "I was forgiven."
I said: "With what did you escape?"
He said: "With [the saying] Lā Ḥawla wa lā quwata illā billāh[82]."
I said: "How did you find your knowledge? I mean the prose, literature and poetry?"
He said: "I found that like scattered dust[83]."

81 Meaning that the remembrance of Allah was what really beneficial
82 "There is no power to move and no strength except with Allah"
83 A Quranic term referring to how big hard deep-rooted mountains become like dust, scattered by the wind

With this same narration to Ahmad ibn 'Alī ibn Thābit who said: "Abu al-Ḥasan Muhammad ibn al-Muẓaffar recited unto us, he said Abu Bakr Ahmad ibn Sulaymān al-Najjār recited unto us that Hilāl ibn al-'Ula recited to us that he said to himself:

A tongue which used to speak expressive words shall wither
O my wish is that on the Day of Display[84] it would be safe!
And what use is the ability to express, if it is not pious
And what harms the pious one if he has a non-expressive tongue

84 Day of Judgement

14

Karāmāt and Gifts of the *'Awlīya'*

Allah – Exalted be He – said:

﴿أَلا إِنَّ أَولِيَاءَ اللهِ لا خَوفٌ عَليهِم ولا هُم يَحزَنُونَ، الَّذِينَ ءامَنُوا وَكَانُوا يَتَّقُونَ، لَهُمُ البُشرَى فِي الحَيَوٰةِ الدُّنيَا وفِي الآخِرَةِ، لا تَبدِيلَ لِكَلِمَـٰتِ اللهِ ذَٰلِكَ هُوَ الفَوزُ العَظِيمُ﴾

﴾Surely, the *'awlīyā'*[85] of Allah will have no fear over them, nor will they grieve. [They are] those who have believed and they were pious. For them, will be the good tidings in this worldly life and in the Hereafter. There is no alteration of the Words of Allah. That is indeed the Great Triumph.﴿[86]

Understand that the path of the people of truth is to affirm the *karāmāt*[87] of the *'awlīyā'*; and that they are continuous occurrences in the different eras. This is proved through the evidence of the intellects, and the explicit transmitted texts.

85 'Awliya' : plural of the word walī: a difficult word to translate. It can be translated as someone who has a wonderful connection with Allah, to the extent that he loves Allah and Allah loves him. He is guided, protected and honoured by Allah. Part of Allah's honour is to bestow on him a karāmāh

86 Holy Quran: Yūnus 10:62-64

87 Linguistically the word karāmah (pl. karāmāt) means a nobility or generous gift. It is simply translated as a miracle: which is an extraordinary and welcome event that is not explicable by natural or scientific laws and is therefore attributed to divine agency. As you shall read in this section that the notion of miracles is not restricted to Prophets, who have two types of miracles: karāmāt and mu'jizāt

As for the evidence of the intellect; then it is something that can happen, and its occurrence does not lead to the annulment of any of the fundamentals of the *dīn*. Thence, it becomes an obligation to describe Allah the Almighty with the ability to do it, and whatever is able to be done, is possible to occur.

As for the narrations: then there are verses in the Great Quran and extensive *aḥadīth*.

As for the verses, the Almighty says in the story of Maryam:

﴿وهُزِّي إِلَيكِ بِجِذعِ النَّخلَةِ تُسَـٰقِط عَلَيكِ رُطَباً جَنِيّاً﴾

﴾And shake toward you the trunk of the palm tree, ripe dates will fall on to you.﴿[88]

Imam Abu al-Ma'ālī – the Imam of the Two Sacred Masjids[89] – (may Allah Almighty have mercy on him) said: Maryam was not a prophet according to the unanimous agreement by the scholars.[90] And similar things were said by others. Rather, she was one of his protected beings, who was truthful, as Allah the Exalted informed us about her.

And the Almighty said:

﴿كُلَّمَا دَخَلَ عَلَيها زَكَرِيَّا المِحرَابَ، وَجَدَ عِندَهَا رِزقاً
قَالَ يَـٰمَريَمُ أَنَّى لَكِ هَذَا قَالَت هُوَ مِن عِندِ اللهِ﴾

﴾Whenever Zakariyyā entered onto her in the *miḥrāb*, he would find with her some provision. He would say, 'Maryam! From where did you get this?' She would say, 'It is from Allah'.﴿[91]

88 Holy Quran: Maryam 19:25
89 This is the famous title given to this great scholar
90 Whilst he may have said that, it is not unanimous; and there are scholars who say that she was a prophet
91 Holy Quran: Family of Imran 3:37

Also, from the story of the companion of Sulaymān ﷺ who said:

﴿أَنَا ءَاتِيكَ بِهِ قَبلَ أَن يَرتَدَّ إِلَيكَ طَرفُكَ﴾

﴿I will bring it to you, before your eyesight returns to you.﴾[92]

The scholars said: "And he was not a prophet."

And of it, that which was inferred by the Imam of the Two Sacred Masjids and others; from that the story of Mūsā's mother.

And of it, that which was deduced by 'Ustādh Abu al-Qāsim al-Qushayrī from the story of Dhul Qarnayn.

Al-Qushayrī and others deduced the same from the story of al-Khiḍr with Mūsā, may Allah's prayers and peace be upon them. They said: "He was not a prophet, rather a *walī*"
However, this is in contrast to the chosen opinion of the majority who said he is a prophet.
It was said: He was a prophet and a messenger.
It was said: He was a *walī*. And it was said: He was an angel.

I have clarified the difference in this matter, and I have explained it in (Tahdhīb al-'Asmā' wa al-Lughāt) and in the explanation of (al-Muhadh-dhab).

And of it [the evidence] is the story of the people of the cave and what it has included of supernatural occurrences. The Imam of the Two Sacred Masjids and others said: "They were not prophets, according to the unanimous opinion."

As for the *aḥadīth*, there are many.

Among them is the hadith of Anas, that two men from the

92 Holy Quran: Chapter of the Ants 27:40

companions of the Prophet ﷺ came out from the presence of the Prophet ﷺ on a dark night, and with them were like two lamps that shone between their hands. When they separated, the light remained with each one of them until they arrived to their families.

Al-Bukhārī included it in his Ṣaḥīḥ in "The Book of Prayer" and in "The Signs of Prophethood".
These two men were 'Abbād ibn al-Bishr and 'Usayd ibn Huḍayr.

And of it is the hadith of the three people of the cave, who retreated to the cave, and a rock which closed their exit! Each one of them prayed with a supplication, and the rock opened up to release them. This has been narrated in Ṣaḥīḥ al-Bukhārī and Muslim.

And of it, is the hadith of Abu Hurayrah ﷺ in the story of Jurayj who said to the breastfeeding boy: "Who is your father?"
He said: "So and so the shepherd!"
This is also narrated in the Ṣaḥīḥ.

Including the hadith of Abu Hurayrah who said: The Prophet ﷺ said: **"Amongst the nations who were before you, there were people who were spoken to. If there is one in my ummah, then it would be 'Omar."**

In another narration:
"There were those who were before you from the Children of Israel who were spoken to, yet they were not prophets...."

Al-Bukhārī narrated this in his Ṣaḥīḥ.

And of it [the evidences] is the famous hadith in Ṣaḥīḥ al-Bukhārī and other books regarding the story of Khubayb al-Ansārī ﷺ the Companion of the Messenger of Allah ﷺ.
The saying of the daughter of al-Ḥārith who said in it: "By Allah, I

have never seen a prisoner who is better than Khubayb. By Allah, I found him one day eating from a bunch of grapes in his hand, whilst he was bound in irons, and there is no fruit in Makkah!" And she used to say: "It is Allah who provided for Khubayb."

The *aḥadīth*, narrations and sayings of the predecessors and the successors - in this section - are more than can be numerated; so it is sufficient with what we have indicated of. And you shall see in this section, sentences indicating that, as well as in the rest of this book, *in sha Allah*.

The response to the Mu'tazilites

Imam Abu al-Ma'ālī - the Imam of the Two Holy Sacred Masjids – said: "What the people of the truth have concluded is the permissibility to break the norms in the case of the *'awliyā'*; and the Mu'tazilites have insisted on denying this.

Then, of the people of the truth who has concluded that the extraordinary dignity which breaks norms; its condition is that it takes place without preference for it or out of choice from the *walī*.

These people have reached the verdict that the *karāmah* differs from the *mu'jizah*[93] from this aspect.

The Imam said: "This statement is incorrect!"

Others have concluded the permissibility of the occurrence of the *karāmah* from the aspect of choosing it; but they refuted it from occurring on the basis of one's claim; so they said: "If the *walī* claimed

93 mu'jizah: it is often translated as a miracle, however according to the Islamic understanding, a mu'jizah is a miracle which is presented by a prophet, and it exhausts the opponent in being able to match it or explain it away

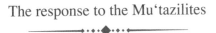

the *wilāyah*[94], and he used to prove his claim in a way that violates the norms, then that is rejected."

These people distinguished the *karāmah* and *mu'jizah* from this aspect. He [the Imam] said: "This method is not satisfactory – also."

He went on: "In our position, the emergence of supernatural occurrences happening with a possible claim, is not refuted."

He said: "Some of our companions have come to the conclusion that what happened as a *mu'jizah* for a Prophet cannot be judged to occur as a *karāmah* for a *walī*."

So, according to this group, it is not possible as a *karāmah* for a *walī* to split the sea or to change the staff into a snake, or resurrect the dead among other things which were signs for Prophets.

The Imam said: "This method is not correct - also."

He said: What is acceptable to us is the permissibility of paranormal events in the display of *karāmāt*. He said: Our purpose in invalidating these doctrines and opinion is to prove what we hold as correct."

He said: "As for the difference between a *mu'jizah* and *karāmah*; then they do not differ – in the possibility of occurrence rationally, except that the occurrence of the *mu'jizah* is in accordance with the prophecy claim, and the *karāmah* occurs without claiming prophecy."

The Imam said: "There have been signs which have taken place during the birth of the Messenger of Allah ﷺ which no one attributed to Islam can deny, and that was before the prophethood and the mission."

94 The noun for the state of becoming a walī

And the *mu'jizah* does not precede the claim of prophecy, so it was a *karāmah*.

He said: "If an unreasoned claimant claims that the signs which we have inferred were *mu'jizāt* for a prophet of every age, then that is him storming into ignorance. For, if we search in the previous eras, we do not find the signs that we adhered to, being coupled with the claim of prophecy, nor did it occur because of someone making a challenge.

If they said: 'It occurred for the prophets, not for their commoners.' we say: 'The condition of a *mu'jizah* is the claim; if it is missing, then it is a supernatural occurrence, as a *karāmah* for the Prophets, and we make it our purpose to prove the *karāmāt*', and there was no prophet at the time of the birth of our Prophet Muhammad ﷺ which the signs can be based upon.

The Imam said: "Thence, the *karāmāt* have been clarified, as being possible and permissibly occurring from textual and rational perspectives."

Difference between magic and a *karāmah*

The Imam and others have said in the difference between magic and *karāmah* that magic does not appear except from a transgressor.

He said: "This is not derived from the rational conclusion of the mind, but taken from the consensus of the *Ummah*."

The Imam said: "Then, a *karāmah*, even if it does not appear in relation to a transgressor who is open with his immorality; does not bear witness to the *wilāyah* with certainty. For, if you witnessed to such, then its owner would have security from the consequences; and that is not permissible for a *walī* in regards to a *karāmah* by agreement."

This is the last words of Imam of the Two Sacred Masjids.

The Imam 'Ustādh Abu al-Qāsim al-Qushayrī, may Allah Almighty have mercy on him, said (in what we have been narrated to in his Message):

"The appearance of *karāmāt* is a sign of the sincerity of those who it appeared to in his conditions. Whoever is not sincere, the appearance of the *karāmāt* is not permissible."

[He said]: "A *karāmah* must be an act that contradicts the norm during the days of burdening (*taklīf*), apparently on someone who carries a description of *wilāyah*, in the sense of believing it in its condition."

Difference between *mu'jizah* and a *karāmah*

He said: "The people of truth spoke about the difference between a *karāmah* and a *mu'jizah*.

Imam Abu Iṣhāq al-Asfarīnī, may Allah Almighty have mercy on him, said:
"*Mu'jizāt* are indications of the truthfulness of prophets; and the evidence of prophecy is found only with a prophet."

And he used to say: The *'awlīya'* have *karāmāt*, including answering of the *du'ā'*; as for the category of what is for the prophets, then no."

Imam Abu Bakr ibn Fūrak (may Allah Almighty have mercy on him) said:

"*Mu'jizāt* are indications of honesty. If the owner claims prophethood, then it is proof of his truth. Whilst, if the owner referred to it as the state of *wilāyah*, then it is indicative of his truthfulness in this condition. In this case, it is called *karāmah* and not *mu'jizah*, even if it is of the same type as the *mu'jizāt*, due to the difference.

And he - may Allah have mercy on him, used to say: "The difference between *mu'jizāt* and *karāmāt* is that the Prophets (peace and prayers be upon them) are commanded to show them; whereas the *walī* is obligated to veil it and conceal it. And, the Prophet claims prophethood and affirms it with the *mu'jizah*; whereas the *walī* does not claim it and does not affirm his *karāmah*, as it is possible that this (*karāmah*) is a plot.[95]"

The unique sensation of his time in his field Judge Abu Bakr al-Bāqilānī ؎ said:"*Mu'jizāt* are specific to Prophets. *Karāmāt* are for *'awlīyā'* just as they are for Prophets. It is not considered a *mu'jiazh* for the *'awlīyā'*, as the condition of the *mu'jizah* is that it is coupled with Prophethood.

The *mu'jizah* is not a *mu'jizah* for its actual act; rather, it was a *mu'jizah* because it contains many descriptions. Whenever a condition of those is defective, then it isn't a *mu'jizah*, and one of these conditions is the claim of prophethood. And the *walī* doesn't claim prophethood, so that which is displayed from him is not a *mu'jizah*."

Al-Qushayrī said: "And this what he has said is what we adopt and what we say; rather we account ourselves before Allah. All or most of the conditions of *mu'jizāt* are found in the *karāmah* except for this one condition, which is the claim of prophethood. So, the *mu'jizah* is not a *karāmah*."

The *karāmah* like the *mu'jizah* is an act of Allah, no doubt. It is created and not ancient; and it is supernatural and not affirmed to

---

95 By "plot", he is referring to the unseen purpose behind this gift; for it may be that Allah chooses to test people by giving them things to see how they would behave

custom. It occurs at the time of *taklīf*[96] for a slave, as a speciality for him and giving him preference.

It may happen by choosing and asking for it; but it also may not. And it may be without his choice on most occasions.

The *walī* is not commanded to call the creation to himself; yet if that did appear from someone who is eligible for it, it is accepted. The people of the truth differed in regards to the *walī*: is it permissible for him to know that he is a *walī* or not?

Imam Abu Bakr ibn Fūrak (may Allah have mercy on him) said: "It is not permissible, because this will strip him of fear and thus necessitate safety."

'Ustādh Abu 'Alī Al-Daqqāq - may Allah have mercy on him - used to say that it is possible; and that saying is what we give preference to and say [also].

This is not a necessity for all *'awlīyā'* such that not every *walī* should know if he is a *walī*. But it is possible that some of them would know, whilst others would not.

If anyone of them knew that he was a *walī*, then his knowing of this is a unique *karāmah* for him.

Not all *karāmāt* should be the same for all *'awlīyā'*. Indeed, if a *walī* does not have an apparent *karāmah* in this *dunyā*, the absence of it does not in any way slur him from being a *walī*.

This is in contrast to the Prophets, for it is mandated for them to have *mu'jizāt*, as the Prophet is sent to the creation; and people are in need to know his truthfulness, and this would not be known without a *mu'jizah*.

96 This is the state in which one can understands the laws and their application

The state of a *walī* is opposite of that, because it is not obligated for the creation, nor for the *walī* [himself] to know that he is a *walī*.

The ten companions ﷺ believed the Messenger ﷺ as he informed them that they are of the People of *Jannah*.

As for the saying of the one who says it is not permissible, because it removes them out of fear, then there is nothing wrong with them not being afraid of the change of consequences. And that which they find in their hearts of prestige, glorification, and reverence for the Truth ﷻ is more and rises above much of fear.

'Ustādh al-Qushayrī said:"Know that the *walī* should not feel comfort towards the *karāmah* that appears on him, nor should he have any observation of it. Rather, the appearance of the like should result in a strengthening in certainty and an increase in insight, as they determine the correctness of what they have of doctrines, and Allah knows best."

Karāmāt of a *walī* are *mu'jizah* of the Prophet

Al-Qushayrī - may Allah have mercy on him - said: "If it said: 'How is it permissible to display these *karāmāt* which have excess over the *mu'jizāt* of the Apostles?'

We say: 'These *karāmāt* follow the *mu'jizāt* of our Prophet Muhammad ﷺ, because everyone who is not true in Islam, the *karāmāt* will be prevented from him. For every Prophet, whom one of his *ummah* has displayed a *karāmah*, then it is counted amongst his miracles. For, had that Messenger not been true, then the *karāmah* would not feature on one of those who followed him: meaning the *karāmah* for that individual'."

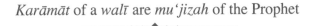

The *Walī* may not be preferred over the Prophet

Al-Qushayrī said: "Is it permissible to prefer a *walī* over a Prophet?

We said: "The rank of the *'awlīyā'* does not reach the rank of the Prophets - peace and prayers be upon them, as the consensus is held on that."

'Ustādh al-Qushayrī (may Allah have mercy on him) said: "These *karāmāt* may be an answering of a *du'ā'*; or it may be bringing food during famine without an apparent reason; or getting water at times of drought, or facilitating the travel of a distance in a short time; or the ridding of an enemy; or hearing a message from a [distant] caller; as well as other supernatural acts."

He said: "And you must know that many capabilities are known today with certainty that they are not permissible to occur as *karāmāt* for *awlīyā'*. This is known by necessity or near necessity. This includes:

A - Bringing forth a human without parents

B - Changing an inanimate object to a creature.

As well as many other examples."

Derivation of the word *walī*

Al-Qushayrī said: The [word] *walī* may originate from two [roots]:

1 - One of them is the derivation of the root fa'īl (فَعيل) which is an exaggerated form of the fā'il (فاعل) (subject); similar to the word 'alīm (عليم) is to 'ālim (عالم); and qadīr (قدير) is to qādir (قادر).

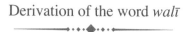

In this sense, its meaning will be: the one whom his obedience is in ongoing succession without being disrupted with any sin.

2 - The second [derivation] is fa'īl (فَعيل) meaning maf'ūl (مفعول) (object); like qatīl (قتيل) means maqtūl (مقتول) and jarīḥ (جريح) meaning majrūḥ (مجروح).

In this sense, its meaning will be the one who Allah takes care of his preservation and guarding, perpetually and in succession.

Such then, He does not create for him the disregard which is the ability to do an act of disobedience; rather He sustains his success, which is the ability to do an act of obedience.

Allah the Almighty said:

﴿وَهُوَ يَتَوَلَّى الصَّـٰلِحِينَ﴾

﴿And He takes care of the righteous﴾[97]

Usage of the term "righteous slave" (العبد الصالح); is used for both a Prophet and a *walī*

Allah Almighty said:

﴿وَإِسمَـٰعِيلَ وَإِدرِيسَ وَذَا الكِفلِ كُلٌّ مِنَ الصَّـٰبِرِينَ
وَأَدخَلنَـٰهُم فِي رَحمَتِنَا إِنَّهُم مِنَ الصَّـٰلِحِينَ﴾

﴿And Ismā'īl, 'Idrīs, and Dhal Kifl: they are all of the patient. And We entered them into Our Mercy: they are of the *ṣāliḥīn* (righteous)﴾[98]

97 Holy Quran: Chapter of the Heights 7:196
98 Holy Quran: Chapter of the Prophets 21:85-86

The Almighty said of the Prophet Yaḥyā:

﴿وَنَبِيًّا مِنَ الصَّٰلِحِينَ﴾

﴾And a Prophet of the *ṣāliḥīn* (righteous)﴿[99]

The Almighty said:

﴿فَأُولَٰئِكَ مَعَ الَّذِينَ أَنْعَمَ اللَّهُ عَلَيْهِم مِنَ النَّبِيِّينَ وَالصِّدِّيقِينَ وَالشُّهَدَاءِ وَالصَّٰلِحِينَ﴾

﴾Those are the ones whom Allah has blessed them, among the Prophets, the sincerely truthful, the martyrs and the ṣāliḥīn (righteous)﴿[100]

In the authentic hadith that the Prophet ﷺ said in regards to AbdUllah ibn 'Omar that "**He is a *ṣāliḥ* (righteous) man**". And the verses and *aḥadīth* in the sense of what I mentioned are many.

As for the definition of the *ṣāliḥ* (righteous), then Imam Abu 'Isḥāq al-Zajjāj said in his book The Meanings of the Qur'an, and Abu 'Isḥāq Ibn Qarqūl, the author of "The Essences of Lights":

"He is the one who is established in what is necessitated of him regarding the rights of Allah Almighty; and the slaves."

Difference between infallibility and preservation

Imam al-Qushayrī said: "If it is said: 'Is the *walī* infallible or not?'

We say, as for that being obligated, like it is said in the [right] of the Prophets: then no. And as for him to be preserved so that it

99 Holy Quran: Chapter of the Family of Imran 3:39
100 Holy Quran: Chapter of the Women 4:69

does not insist on sins, even if some shortfalls occur from him at times, or errors, then this is not curtailed from their description."

It was said to al-Junayd: "Does the *'Ārif* commit adultery?"
He lowered his head for a short while, then raised his head and said: "And the matter of Allah will be a pre-set fixed destiny."

Fear does not depart from the *'awliyā'*

Al-Qushayrī - may Allah have mercy on him – said, "If it is said: 'Does the fear vanish from the *'awlīyā'?'*. We say: The predominant feature of the seniors is fear. And that which was aforementioned is more of a rarity, yet it is not refuted."

And this is al-Sarī al-Saqatī ﷺ who says: "If one were to enter a garden in which there are many trees, and on every tree there is a bird who says [to him] with an eloquent tongue: 'Peace be upon you, O *walī* of Allah!' and yet, he doesn't fear that this may be a plot, then he has fallen to the plot."

The likes of these narrations are many.
He said: "If it is said: 'Is it permissible for the *walī* to distance the fear of deception?'

We say: If he is absorbed in what he is witnessing, abducted from sensing his condition, then he is free from that in which has overcome him. Whilst fear is the quality of those who are present."

The predominant state of the *walī* when he is alert

Al-Qushayrī said: If it is said: What is the predominant state of the *walī* during his alertness?

We say:

1 - His sincerity in the performance of the duties towards Allah Almighty

2 - His compassion and gentleness for creation in all his states

3 - Extension of his mercy to all creation

4 - His continuous enduring from others [their issues] with a beautiful character

5 - His initiation to seek goodness from Allah Exalted towards them without asking anything from them

6 - Suspension of his concern in regards to saving the creation; and to abstain from seeking revenge from them

7 - Being aware of sensing his right over them, along with having a short arm in regards to their wealth / property

8 - Leaving greed in every facet, and holding back the tongue from extending it with badness towards them

9 - Avoidance of witnessing their badness; and to avoid becoming an opponent in this dunyā or the hereafter.

I said: It means that he pardons them in regards to his rights in the *dunyā*, such that he does not seek it from them; and thus he has nothing left to claim for in the hereafter.

Allah the Almighty said:

﴿وَلَمَن صَبَرَ وَغَفَرَ إِنَّ ذَٰلِكَ لَمِنْ عَزْمِ الْأُمُورِ﴾

﴿And for those who are patient and forgive, this is of the resolve of matters﴾[101]

101 Holy Quran: Chapter of the Consultation 42:43

And Allah the Almighty said:

﴿وَالكَـٰظِمِينَ الغَيظَ وَالعَافِينَ عَنِ النَّاسِ وَاللهُ يُحِبُّ المُحسِنِينَ﴾

﴿And those who hold back anger, and pardon people; and Allah loves those who are righteous﴾[102]

We have been narrated to in the book of 'Amal al-yawm wa al-Laylah[103] by Ibn al-Sunnī with his chain of transmission to Anas ﷺ that the Messenger of Allah ﷺ said:

"Are any of you unable to be like Abu Ḍamḍam?!"

They said: "And who is Abu Ḍamḍam, O Messenger of Allah?

He said:

"He used to say when he woke up: 'Oh Allah, I endow myself and my honour to You.' Such that he does not insult those who insult him; and he does not wrong those who have wronged him; and he does not strike those who hit him."

I said: it means that he does not seek recompense from those who have wronged him, as Allah Almighty said:

﴿فَمَنِ اعتَدَى عَلَيكُم فَاعتَدُوا عَلَيهِ بِمِثلِ مَا اعتَدَى عَلَيكُم﴾

﴿Whoever transgresses against you, then you can transgress against him in the same way as he transgressed against you﴾[104]

Al-Qushayrī said: "Know that amongst the greatest of *karāmāt* - that are for *'awlīyā'* – is the continuation of being helped towards obedience, and protection from sins and violations."

I said: violations include matters that are not sins, like *makrūh* acts which are disliked; and like leaving desires that are recommended to abandon.

102 Holy Quran: Chapter of the Family of Imran 3:134
103 The Book of the Actions of the Day and Night
104 Holy Quran: Chapter of the Cow 2:194

Seeing Allah Almighty

Al-Qushayrī said: "If it is said: 'Is it permissible to see Allah - Blessed and Exalted – with the eyesight today in the *dunyā* from an aspect of *karāmah*?'

We said: The strongest [opinion] is that it is not permissible, for the attainment of consensus in this matter."

He said: "And I heard Imam Abu Bakr ibn Fūrak ﷺ talking about Abu al-Ḥasan al-'Ash'arī (may Allah have mercy on him) that he said: 'There are two sayings' in the Book "Al-Ru'yah al-Kabīr". I said: A group have conveyed the consensus that seeing Allah Almighty does not occur for the *'awlīyā'* in the *dunyā*, not because it is not possible; for it is possible according to the rationality with the people of the truth.

The companions and those who came after them differed in regards to the seeing of the Prophet ﷺ his Lord Glorified and Exalted on the Night of 'Isrā'; and the choice of most is that he did see Him; and that is the view of Ibn 'Abbās – may Allah be pleased with them both. I have expanded the purposes of this in the beginning of the explanation of Ṣaḥīḥ Muslim - may Allah have mercy on him.

Can the state of *Wilāyah* be withdrawn?

Al-Qushayrī said: "If it is said: 'Is it possible that one is a *walī* in his state and then his end changes?'

We say that whoever has made among the conditions of *wilāyah* the good consequence, then it is not possible. And whoever says that he is in that state a believer of the reality, and it is permissible for his state to change, then it is not distant that he is a *walī* in that state as a true believer, then he changes."

He said: "This is what we choose, and it may be from among the general *karāmāt* of the *walī* to know that he is safe in his consequence, and that his ending will not change; so this issue will be attached to what we aforementioned that the *walī* may know that he is a *walī*."

As for the *karāmāt*, then we have mentioned previously its definition. And as for *mawāhib*, it is the plural of *mawhibah*. A *mawhibah* is not an extraordinary thing, but it is usually a little far fetched under normal circumstances. It is distinguished for some people, and this is not specific to the *'awlīyā'*, but rather for them and others.
And I will mention in the next section a collection of *karāmāt* and approved *mawāhib*, *in sha Allah*, Exalted be He.

Allah Almighty has said:

﴿وَكُلًّا نَّقُصُّ عَلَيكَ مِن أَنبَاءِ الرُّسُلِ مَا نُثَبِّتُ بِهِ فُؤَادَكَ﴾

﴿And such: We narrate on to you of the news of the Apostles which We strengthen with it your heart.﴾[105]

The Almighty said:

﴿أُولَئِكَ الَّذِينَ هَدَى اللهُ فَبِهُدَاهُمُ اقتَدِه﴾

﴿Such are those whom Allah has guided; so in their guidance, follow.﴾[106]

105 Holy Quran: Chapter of Hūd 9:120
106 Holy Quran: Chapter of The Cattle 6:90

Our Shaykh the Righteous Imam and Judge Abu Muhammad Abdul Raḥmān the son of the Shaykh and righteous imam Abu 'Omar ibn Ahmad ibn Muhammad ibn Ahmad ibn Qudāmah who said: Abu Hafs 'Omar ibn Muhammad ibn Mu'ammar ibn Tabarazad narrated to us that Abu al-Fatḥ Abdul Malik ibn Abi al-Qasim al-Karūkhī narrated to us that Abu 'Āmir Maḥmūd ibn al-Qasim ibn Muhammad al-'Azdī and Abu Bakr Ahmad ibn Abdul Ṣamad al-Khazrajī and Abu Nasr Abdul Azīz ibn 'Omar al-Rafānī narrated to us saying: Abu Muhammad Abdul Jabbār ibn Muhammad ibn AbdUllah ibn al-Jarrāḥ al-Jarāḥī narrated to us that he said: Abu al-'Abbās Muhammad ibn Ahmad ibn Maḥbūb al-Maḥbūbī narrated to us that he said: Imam Abu 'Isā al-Tirmidhī narrated to us that he said 'Omar ibn Ḥafṣ al-Shaybānī narrated to us that AbdUllah ibn Wahb from 'Amr ibn al-Hārith from Darrāj from Abu al-Haytham from Abu Sa'īd al-Khudrī ﵁ from the Messenger of Allah ﷺ that he said:
"The believer will never be full in regards to the goodness he hears, until his end is *Jannah*."

Al-Tirmidhī said: "This is a sound hadith."

With this chain of transmission to al-Tirmidhī, who said: 'Alī ibn Ḥajar narrated to us that he said: Muslim ibn 'Amr narrated to us that he said: " 'Omar ibn Hānī' used to pray every day a thousand prostrations - meaning a thousand rak'ahs - and glorify [Allah] one hundred thousand times [i.e. saying Subḥān Allah].

Stories and Narrations of the Righteous

Abu Muslim al-Khawlānī ⁂

Our Shaykh Abu al-Baqā' the Hadith Master informed us that he said that Abu Muhammad narrated to us that Abu Bakr narrated to us that al-Khatīb, narrated to us that al-Ḥasan ibn Muhammad al-Bazzāz narrated to us that Muhammad ibn Jaʿfar al-'Ādami narrated to us that Muhammad ibn Mūsā al-Shattūbī narrated to us that Hārūn ibn Maʿrūf narrated to us that Ḍamurah narrated to us from 'Othman from 'Atā' from his father who said: Abu Muslim's [al-Khawlānī] wife said: "O Abu Muslim! We don't have any flour."

He said: "Do you have anything?"

She said: "A dirham, which we got from selling some yarn."

He said: "Give it to me, and give me the sack."

So he entered the market, and stood in front of a man selling food. A beggar stood near him. The beggar said, "O Abu Muslim, give me some charity!"

So, Abu Muslim ran away and went to another stall; but the beggar followed him saying, "Give me charity!"

So, when he wore him down [with his persistent asking], he gave him the dirham.
He, then took the sack and filled it with carpenters' sawdust and earth.
Then, he came to the door of his house and knocked on the door, and his heart was terrified of his family.
When she opened the door, he threw the sack and went.
When she opened it, she found white refined flour, she kneaded and baked it.
Then when a portion of the night passed, Abu Muslim came and knocked on the door; his heart fearful. When he entered, she put before him a tray with white loaves of bread.
He said: "From where did you get this from?"
She said: "O Abu Muslim! It is of the flour that you brought!"
So, he started to eat whilst crying!

I said: What a precious story this is! And how enumerate its benefits are!

As for Abu Muslim, the owner of this *karāmah* ﷺ his name is: AbdUllah ibn Thuwab, or it is said: Ibn Thawāb, or Ibn Athwab, or Ibn AbdUllah or ibn 'Awf or Ibn Yaslam. It is also suggested his name was Ya'qūb ibn Awf. The correct of which is what we mentioned at the beginning.

He is from the people of Yemen, who inhabited the Levant in Dāriyā: the renowned village next to Damascus. He was among the senior followers, and amongst their most worshipping and righteous. He is one of those who have apparent *karāmāt* in the dramatically recurring Sunni states.

He had travelled to the Messenger of Allah ﷺ to accompany him; yet the Prophet ﷺ died whilst he was still in the journey. So, he came and met Abu Bakr al-Ṣiddīq, 'Omar and other companions ﷺ.

Among the *karāmāt* of Abu Muslim ﷺ

Among his precious *karāmāt* is what was narrated by Imam Ahmad ibn Ḥanbal, may Allah be pleased with him in his book of al-Zuhd is that Abu Muslim al-Khawlānī passed by the Tigris whilst it was breaking the wood from its banks, so he walked on water and then turned to his companions saying: "Do you miss any of your equipment, so you can ask Allah ﷻ?"

And he narrated it from another path [of transmission], in it: it is stated that he stood on the [bank of] Tigris, then he praised Allah Almighty and glorified Him. Then he mentioned His blessings, and mentioned the crossing of the Children of Israel in the sea. He then advanced his horse, so it moved entering the Tigris; and the people followed him, until the people crossed. May Allah be pleased with him.

Also, with the transmission of Imam Ahmad (may Allah have mercy on him): that Abu Muslim was in the land of the Romans, so the governor sent an army, and he had set a time for their return. So they were late, which caused Abu Muslim to be concerned for their delay. So, whilst he was doing ablution on the shore of a river and he was speaking to himself in regards to their matter, a crow landed on a tree across from him. The crow said, "O Abu Muslim! Are you worried about the army?"
He said: "Yes."
The crow said: "Do not worry; for they have been victorious and they will return to you on such and such a day at such and such time."
Abu Muslim said to him: "Who are you, may Allah have mercy on you?"
He said: "I am one who brings happiness to the hearts of believers."
Then, the regiment arrived at the specified time, as was mentioned.

And with the authority of Ahmad ﷺ that Abu Muslim was sitting and talking with his companions in the land of the Romans. They said: "O Abu Muslim! We are craving some meat, so if you ask Allah Almighty that He may provide us with some."
He said: "O Allah! You have heard their saying, and You are able to do what they have requested!"
It was only then that they heard some shouting in the military camp; and they saw a stag which had entered and passed by the companions of Abu Muslim. So, they jumped up and caught it.

Also, according to the authority of Ahmad (may Allah be pleased with him) that a famine befell the people during the era of Mu'āwiyah ﷺ. So Mu'āwiyah went out with the people to ask for rain. When they arrived the prayer area, Mu'āwiyah said to Abu Muslim: "You have seen what has befallen the people, So pray to Allah!"
He said: "I will do so."
So, he mounted a she-camel and stood on its back, and he uncovered his head from his *burnus*[107] and raised his arms, and then said: "Oh Allah! We surely seek the rain from You. And I have come to you announcing my sins, so do not disappoint me!"
So, they did not move, until they were watered.
Abu Muslim then said: "O Allah! Mu'āwiyah has placed me in a place of boasting; so if I have any good with You, take me to You!"
This was on the Thursday, and Abu Muslim died on the following Thursday: ﷺ.

With the transmission of Hadith Master Abu Ṭāhir al-Silafī, from Sharḥabīl Ibn Muslim that when al-Aswad Ibn Qays al-'Anasī the Liar claimed prophethood in Yemen, he sent to Abu Muslim al-Khawlānī. When he came to him, he said: "Do you bear witness that I am the Messenger of Allah?"
Abu Muslim said: "I can't hear!"

107 A garment which has a hood attached to it

He said: "Do you bear witness that Muhammad is the Messenger of Allah?"
He said: "Yes."
He – then – repeated the question, and Abu Muslim repeated his answers.
Al-Aswad ordered that a great fire be lit and stoked!
He then threw Abu Muslim in it, yet it did not harm him.
It was suggested to al-Aswad to exile Abu Muslim or else he will corrupt those who follow you, so he ordered him to leave.
Abu Muslim came to al-Madinah, and the Messenger of Allah ﷺ had passed away; and Abu Bakr ﷺ had succeeded him.
Abu Muslim tied his mount at the door of the Masjid. He stood up praying in front of one of the pillars of the Masjid. He was spotted by 'Omar who approached him.
He said: "Who is the man?"
He said, "From the people of Yemen."
He said: "Perhaps you are the one whom the Liar burnt with fire?"
He said: "That is AbdUllah ibn Thuwab."
He said: "I ask you by Allah: Is it you?"
He said: "By Allah: yes!"

'Omar then embraced him and wept. He then took him and seated him between him and Abu Bakr ﷺ. He then said, "Praise be to Allah who did not take my life before showing me amongst the nation of Muhammad ﷺ someone who had the same done to him as was done to the Khalīl of al-Raḥmān:[108] 'Ibrāhīm ﷺ."

I said: This is from the most noble of *karāmāt*, and the most precious of illuminating states.

His saying: "I can't hear!" There are two possible aspects: one of which means: I do not accept, and the second: that it is as is outwardly meant,

108 Close friend – or beloved

that Allah closed his ears from hearing such false obscenity. Some imams have limited this to the first aspect, and to me, the second possibility is more apparent.

Abdul Wāḥid ibn Zayd

Ahmad ibn Abi al-Ḥawārī said in his Book of al-Zuhd that Abu Sulaymān narrated to me that: Abdul Wāḥid ibn Zayd ﷺ, was afflicted by a stroke. So, he asked Allah Almighty to release it from him during times of ablution. So, when the time of ablution came, he would rise from his bed until he went to perform ablution; and when he returned to his bed, the paralysis [from the stroke] would return to him. And Allah knows best.

Sahl ibn AbdUllah

We have been narrated to as in our previous chain to al-Qushayrī (may Allah have mercy on him) that he said: I heard Abu Ḥātim al-Sijistānī say: I heard Abu Naṣr al-Sarrāj say: "We entered Tustur, so we saw in the palace of Sahl ibn AbdUllah – may Allah have mercy on him – a room that people used to call the room of the predators. So, we asked people about that. They said: 'The predators would come to Sahl, and he would receive them in this room, hosting them and feeding them meat, then he would let them go!' Abu Naṣr said: I saw the people of Tustur all of them agreeing on this and they are a lot of people.

Abu al-Khayr al-Tīnātī

And with this chain to al-Qushayrī, who said: I heard Muhammad ibn Ahmad al-Tamimi say: I heard AbdUllah ibn 'Alī al-Ṣūfī say: I heard Ḥamzah ibn AbdUllah al-'Alawī say: "I entered on to Abu al-Khayr al-Tīnātī – may Allah have mercy on him – and I had [within my mind] committed to myself that I would give him salam and leave, and not to eat food with him.

So, when I came out of his house and walked a distance, he was behind me, carrying a plate of food and said: "O young man! Eat of this, for this hour, you are no longer bound by your commitment!"

He said: Abu al-Khayr is famous for his *karāmāt*.

It has been narrated that 'Ibrāhīm al-Raqqī said: I intended him to give him salam. So, he prayed Salatul Maghrib, and he did not recite al-Fātiḥah evenly!

So I said to myself: 'My travel has gone to waste!'

After I gave him salam, I went out for my purification and a lion sought me. So, I returned to him and told him, "The lion has sought me!"

So, he went out and shouted at the lion and said: "Did I not tell you that you should not approach my guests?!"

The lion stepped away, and I purified myself.

Then, when I returned to him, he said: "You were concerned with correcting the outwards, and so you feared the lion. Whilst we were occupied with correcting the hearts, so the lion feared us."

I said: someone who tries to imitate the jurists – and yet has no fiqh – may be deceived in thinking that the prayer of Abu al-Khayr was void, due to the narrator's saying, 'he did not recite al-Fātiḥah evenly!'

This is the ignorance and stupidity of those who are confused by that, and an audacity from him to send suspicions to the *'awliyā'* of the Most Merciful.

Let the sane person be wary of objecting to any of that. Rather, it is his duty if he does not understand their learned wisdom, and their renewed points of reflection, to try to understand it from those who know them.
And everything that you see of this kind: of which those who have no research capabilities assume that they are violations, they are not. Rather the actions of *'awlīyā'* of Allah the Almighty must be interpreted appropriately.

As for this incident, then the answer to this is from three aspects:
The first: It does not invalidate the prayer, by agreement.
The second: He is subdued to that due to a defect in his tongue, and so his prayer was valid, by agreement.
The third: that if he had no excuse, then reciting al-Fātihah is not conditional with Abu Ḥanīfah and a group of scholars, and this *walī* does not have to adhere to the school of those who have obliged it [in the *salah*].

I saw that in the handwriting of the Shaykh ﷺ.

16

Tales which are enjoyable to hear

I have collated the *karāmāt* for some men; and I have made for each one of them a purpose, so that it can be easier to attain, and easier to review and more compelling in the soul of the reader.

You must know that this section – even though it is not one of the chapters of asceticism – it is what the soul relaxes with should it become bored. The ascetic may need the stories of others which do not affect the asceticism and may not be understood comprehensively.

For it may be that they may talk about the affairs of people and the gossip may drag them to talk about forbidden matters of backbiting and the like.

If they become occupied with this, their souls become revitalised when they hear them; and they become occupied with it rather than the ugly matters.

And despite this, these tales that I mention – *in sha Allah* - are not void of benefits that the seeker of the Hereafter will benefit from - and Allah grants success.

Sulaymān ibn Ḥarb and Al-Ma'mūn

We have been narrated to from the authority of Imam Abu Ḥātim al-Rāzī – who is one of the pillars of hadith [narration] who said: "I attended the gathering of Sulaymān ibn Ḥarb (may Allah have mercy on him) in Baghdad. They estimated the number of people who attended his sitting to be forty thousand men.

His gathering was at the palace of al-Ma'mūn. Something similar to a pulpit was built for him and Sulaymān ascended.

Al-Ma'mūn was high in his palace, and the palace door was opened, and a curtain was veiling him, whilst he was writing what Sulaymān dictated.

Abu Ḥātim said that he was not asked about any hadith except that he would narrate it to those who heard.

Judge Abu AbdUllah al-Muḥāmilī

Abu Sa'īd al-Sam'ānī said that the number of those who attended the dictation sitting of Imam Judge Abu AbdUllah al-Muḥāmilī was ten thousand men.

Shihāb al-Dīn al-Suhrawardī and Jamāl al-Dīn

I saw with the Shaykh's handwriting – may Allah have mercy on him – in varied places: I heard our Shaykh and Master the Imam Hadith Master Zain Uddin ﷺ twice, the last of which was on the Wednesday, the 3rd of the holy month of Ramadan in the year 657, in which he says:

The Noble Shaykh Shihāb al-Dīn al-Suhrawardī ﷺ preached in Damascus - may Allah the Exalted protect it and preserve it. The Quran was recited by al-'A'azz ibn 'Ibrāhīm ibn Muhammad al-Mamdūḥ ibn 'Alī al-Rabīnī ibn AbdUllah al-Jawād ibn Ja'far; the Shaykh felt inspired and so took off his clothes. Jamāl al-Dīn bought them for five hundred dirhams, for the blessings.
And he ﷺ did not used to waste any of his time. Rather, he continued to be engaged in prayer, recitation and remembrance ﷺ.
Our Sheikh ﷺ wore of these clothes a rag, and accompanied him for a while in Baghdad in Ribāt ﷺ.

Hadith Master Abdul Ghanī

I heard our Shaykh and Master the Aware Imam, the Remnant of Seniors of the path Sharaf al-Dīn Abu Ismā'īl Muhammad ibn 'Ibrāhīm ibn Ṣarī ibn Hirmās ibn Najjār ibn 'Aqīl ibn Jābir ibn Hikām ibn Hikmah ibn Yusuf ibn Ja'far al-Ṭayyār ibn Abi Tālib.

This ancestry of his; he dictated to me on Friday the fourteenth of Ramadan, 659AH in al-Rawaḥiyyah School in Damascus, may Allah Almighty protect and preserve it. I heard him convey from Shaykh al-Faqīh the righteous Imam Muhammad al-Birsī, who said: "We were waiting for Hadith Master Abdul Ghanī and we were a group, among them there were those who would give fatwa.
So, when he put his foot on the step of the chair, I said [secretly] to myself: 'With what thing has Allah given you virtue over us?'
He turned to me and said: 'O You who has turned away! Whoever serves is served! Whoever serves is served! Whoever serves is served!'
I said: 'I believe in Allah!'

The *Karāmah* of the Compiler of al-Muhadhdhab

I heard our Master Shaykh Kamāl al-Dīn Sallār, may Allah Almighty protect him – recounting from some jurists, that he put the [Book of] al-Muhadhdhab[109] under his head and slept. He had a wet dream. He then commenced to see Abu Isḥāq the compiler of al-Muhadhdhab in the dream, who pushed him with his foot, saying to him, "Wake up! Is it not enough that you have put al-Muhadhdhab under your head, then you became impure."

The *Karāmah* of increasing the few

I heard our Shaykh and Master the Honourable Imam and the brilliant scholar 'Izz al-Dīn Abu Ja'far 'Omar ibn 'Asad ibn Abi Ghālib al-'Ilyī al-Muftī al-Shāfi'ī - may Allah have mercy on him - on the second day of Sha'bān in the year 659AH in al-Rawāḥiyyah School in Damascus, may Allah guard and protect it, and the rest of the abode of Islam and its people: Āmīn.

He saids: "Some of the jurists said: The Shaykh wrote the book "Nihāyat ul-Matlab", and I had the habit of writing a set number of papers at night. So, one night I was writing; and I looked to the lantern and found the amount of oil will not be enough for me to complete my routine writing. Anyhow, I got busy with writing and ignored the lantern. I didn't realise until I had completed my routine writing. I counted the papers. When I finished counting, and mentioned my prayers, I looked at the lantern. As I turned to it, it extinguished suddenly. [or he said something to that effect.]

109 This is the famous fiqh book of Imam al-Shīrāzi (d. 476AH), which is considered an important reference in the Shāfi'ī school

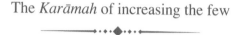

Najm al-Dīn 'Issā al-Kurdī

The Shaykh al-Faqīh Najm al-Dīn 'Isā al-Kurdī al-Shāfi'ī died – may Allah place His Mercy and pleasure on him - in the year 656AH, I think in Sha'bān. He was a faqīh (jurist) at al-Rawāḥiyyah School in the city of Damascus – may Allah protect it, and repel any wrong intender from it; and may Allah preserve and the land of Islam forever, and the entire countries of Islam and their inhabitants.

I saw him in a dream a few days after his death, after the night of Jumu'ah and I knew that he has passed away. I greeted him and said to him: "Have you been resurrected – O Najm al-Dīn – and have you returned?!"

I said to him "Al-Ghazālī said in the chapter on Death in his book 'The Revival of the Sciences of the Dīn':" Death is an enormous experience, and no one has come back to us after death telling us about its reality; only the one who has tasted it knows its reality."

Then, I said, "Tell us about the reality of death!"

He said: "Despite it being hard, it is only a short moment, then it passes…"

I said: "What is your condition after it?"

He said: "There – meaning with Allah – is much goodness."

It is as if he is indicating that his condition is good, due to the virtue of Allah – the Exalted – or as I saw something [to that extent].

Shams al-Dīn Muhammad al-Nawawī

And in this [same] year the Jurist Shams al-Dīn Muhammad al-Nawawī ﷺ passed away. Unto him, I read the honourable full recitation [of the Quran]. I saw him in a dream - may Allah have mercy on him - after his death.

I said: "What is your state O Shams al-Dīn? Are you in *al-Jannah*?" He said, "For now, we do not enter al-Jannah, except after the time of the Hour."
So, I said to him: "True! For the only ones who enter *al-Jannah* now are the Prophets, may Allah's prayers and peace be upon them - and the martyrs. As for others, they will be in bliss, before the Next Life; then they enter *al-Jannah* after the rise of the Hour, as the shari'a has explained."
Then I said to him: "It has been said that the soul returns to the body before the matter of Munkar and Nakīr. So, when does it return to the body? After being placed in the grave or before it whilst the body is in the coffin?"
He said: "After laying in the grave."
May Allah have mercy on him and me, our parents, our shaykhs, and whoever has benefitted us from our companions, and whomever we have offended; and for all other Muslims. Āmīn.

I heard our companion, the Ascetic Imam, the pious knowledgeable aware Shaykh Shams al-Dīn - on Tuesday, the 21st of Jumada al-' Ūlā in the year 661AH, in the Khāniqah al-Shamīṣātiyyah in Damascus - may Allah Almighty protect it – saying: "A few days ago, a dialogue occurred between two shaykhs who were imams, from our companions[110] in front of witnesses, whom he didn't name for me and I prefer not to mention them."

He said, "Between them discussion arose about the Quran that is in the maṣāḥif and the breasts: is it present, but not from the aspect of being omnipresent, as was said by our companions – and that the ink with which it is written is not the ancient words, rather indicative of it.
Then they sought guidance from the Imam of the Two Holy

110 This term usually indicates that they were from the Shāfi'ī school, the same as the two Nawawīs

Sanctuaries[111], to both look at what was mentioned in it, so they looked, then we left.
That night, I saw as if in the midst of a sea there was something, and that thing is what the people wanted. All Muslim scholars surrounding it, looking at that thing, staring at it, not knowing what it is and not being able to realise it.
He said: "I saw the Imam of the Two Sanctuaries enter between the people. He rolled up his garment and entered into that sea about fifteen cubits, then he was not able to reach it! So, he stood there as he was, and the other scholars continued as they were surrounding the sea, looking at that thing.
He said: "And behind the scholars, was an immense number of those who were occupied with the early sciences – I mean the intellectual sciences, such as the science of body and logic, and the principles of the *dīn*. And there were those who were occupied in the matters of argument, who are known for their lack of religion, abstention of salah and bad concepts: and they are those I know!
I saw them all behind the people, and there were dogs that urinated on all of them.
And someone pointed out to me a man – from amongst them, who I know is one of those people of dispute, and was attributed and considered of those lacking dīn. I prefer not to name him. He said: "I saw him drunk!" or as Shams al-*Dīn* said.

We ask Allah Almighty, the Generous, the One who bestows gifts, the One of Greatness and Authority, Virtue and Gratitude, The Merciful, The Compassionate, to improve our end for us, our parents, our shaykhs, our companions, those we love, and all Muslims. Āmīn.

111 Refers to the Sanctuary of Makkah and Madinah

Abu Ya'qūb al-Karrāmī

Al-Sam'ānī mentioned in the Book of Genealogy that the ascetic Abu Ya'qūb Isḥāq ibn Mamshād al-Karrāmī was a good preacher. Five thousand men and women of the people of major sins and from the Magians[112] converted on his hand.[113]

AbdUllah ibn 'Omar ibn Maysar

We have been narrated to from Imam Abu Bakr al-'Anbārī who said: I heard Ahmad ibn Yaḥyā - meaning Abu al-'Abbās - say: "We heard from al-Qawārīrī one hundred thousand hadith."

By al-Qawārīrī, he means AbdUllah ibn 'Omar ibn Maysar - Aba Sa'īd al-Ḥashamī, their *mawla*, al-Baṣrī, then al-Baghdādī.

Shaykh Badr al-Dīn Khalkan al-'Arbīlī

I saw in the handwriting of the Shaykh - may Allah have mercy on him - a comment in separate places: I heard our Shaykh, the Imam and Judge – the aggregate of all sorts of goodness, the remnant of the elders and scholars: Badr al-Dīn Abu AbdUllah Muhammad ibn 'Ibrāhīm ibn Khalkān al-'Arbīlī al-Shāfi'ī ﵀ on Wednesday, the sixteenth of Rajab in the year 660AH, say: "I saw a woman - who I thought he said she is righteous or something to that effect – who memorised the entire Mighty Quran in seventy days!"

112 Magians are an ancient pagan religion who worship fire, known also as Zoroastrians
113 Meaning due to his effort

Kamāl al-Dīn Sallār

I heard our Shaykh the Judge of Islam Kamāl al-Dīn Sallār ﵀ saying: "I memorised the book al-Tanbīh[114] in four months."

The Compilations of Imam al-Ghazālī

I heard our Shaykh al-Batlīsī – may Allah preserve him – several times saying: "I counted the books of al-Ghazālī – may Allah Almighty have mercy on him - which he compiled, and I divided it by his lifespan; so I found that he must have compiled four notebooks every day!"
And that is the Grace of Allah, who directs it as He wills.

Compilations of al-Shāfi'ī and al-'Ash'arī ﵄

I said: Among the most well-known in multitude compilations are our Imam: Imam Abu AbdUllah Muhammad ibn 'Idrīs al-Shāfi'ī and Imam Abu al-Ḥasan al-'Ash'arī – may Allah Almighty be pleased with them both.

Imam Abu Bakr al-Bayhaqī - may Allah have mercy on him – enumerated the works of al-Shāfi'ī.

The Imam and Hadith Master of al-Shām – rather the Hadith Master of the *dunyā* Abu al-Qāsim - known as Ibn 'Asākir ﵀ in his book 'Exposing the lie of the falsifier in what was attributed to Imam Abu al-Ḥasan al-'Ash'arī', counted al-'Ash'arī's compilations to around three hundred.

114 This is the [another] famous fiqh book of Imam al-Shīrāzi (d. 476AH), which is considered an important reference in the Shāfi'ī school

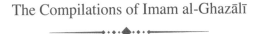

I heard our Shaykh and Master the Noble Imam and Noble Master, the Hadith Master and researcher, and the enlightened auditor, the precise and verifier, the compassionate and righteous, the pious ascetic, and diligent worshiper, the remnant of Hadith Masters, the Mufti, the Shaykh of Imams and Hadith narrators: Ḍiyā Uddīn Abu Isḥāq 'Ibrahīm ibn 'Isā al-Murādī say on the Wednesday 6th of Shawwāl in the year 658AH at al-Bādira'iyyah School in Damascus – may Allah protect and preserve it.

He said: I heard Shaykh Abdul 'Aẓīm, may Allah have mercy on him, saying:

I wrote with my own hands ninety volumes, and I wrote seven hundred chapters, all of which are in the sciences of hadith: compilations and other. And he wrote it from his own compilations, in addition to many other things.

Our Shaykh said: I have not seen nor heard of anyone more diligent than he was in work: he used to be continuous in his work, day and night.

He said: I neighboured him in the School – meaning in Cairo – may Allah protect it. My dwelling was above his dwelling for twelve years. I did not wake up in any hour of the hours of the night, in any of the nights, without finding the light of the lantern lit in his house, and he is occupied with knowledge. And even during mealtimes, the book and the books would be in front of him, as he is occupied with it!

And he further mentioned from his verification, and the intensity of his research and his artistic touches which he was unable to express.

He said: He would hardly go out of the school neither for consolation, nor for celebration, nor for any seeking of comfort, except for Friday prayers. Rather, he would use up all his times in knowledge. May Allah Almighty be pleased with him, with our parents and the Muslims.

I heard our Shaykh Ḍiyā Uddīn ﵀ say: "I wrote Ṣaḥīḥ Al-Bukhārī in six volumes with one pencil, which I used to sharpen. And with that pencil I wrote many things after al-Bukhārī in the City of Cairo – may Allah protect it.

Ibn Qutaybah said in the book "Adab al-Kātib" some words in regards to the Arabic usage of the word "sharpen".

Abu Bakr al-Kittānī

Abu Sa'īd al-Sam'ānī said in the Book of Genealogy: The Shaykh Abu Bakr Muhammad ibn 'Alī ibn Ja'far al-Kittānī completed twelve thousand times [Quran recitation] during the *tawāf*.[115] He died in the year 322AH.

'Izz al-Dīn al-'Irbilī

I heard my Shaykh and Master the Imam Most Learned Scholar, the Mufti, the Verifier, master of precision in all kinds of merits: 'Izz al-Dīn Abu Ḥafṣ 'Omar ibn 'Asad ibn Abi Ghālib al-'Irbilī al-Shāfi'ī t many times, most recently on Friday the 24th of Rajab in the year of 659AH say: "Every worker for Allah ﷻ with obedience, is in remembrance of Allah ﷻ."

Then I saw that transmitted in Sharḥ al-Sunnah by Abu Muhammad al-Baghawī, transmitted from Sa'īd ibn Jubayr ﵁.

Repeat unto me their stories, O Ḥādī[116]
For their tales scour the rusting heart

115 circumambulation around the ka'bah
116 The name of the one who leads the camels in the desert using poems or odes

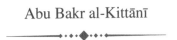

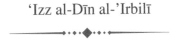

The Book has thus been completed with the Help of Allah and His Support.

This is the last thing that has been found.

And the translation was thus completed on this day the Thursday 9th of Dhul Hijjah 1441AH.

May Allah the Almighty be pleased with its author, the walī of Allah Shaykh Muḥyī Uddin al-Nawawī ﵀; for compiling such a beautiful compilation which is indeed befitting to be a Garden. And May Allah the Exalted extend his pleasure to the translator of his works from Arabic to English: Omer ibn Hasem El-Hamdoon al-Zubaydī al-Barītānī.

And may Allah extend His pleasure to our parents, our shaykhs, our companions and all Muslims, and praise be to Allah alone, and may Allah's prayers be upon our master Muhammad, and upon his good and pure family and great companions.

Glossary of terms

al-Jannah: See Jannah

al-Sāliḥīn: See ṣāliḥīn

'abdāl: *lit*. substitutes or 'replaceables'. They are an elite group of righteous people, who replace one another. It is said that the world will not be void of any one of them at any one time. The notion of their existence is based on a hadith, which the hadith verifiers have disagreed on its authenticity.

'aqīdah: Doctrine or theological beliefs

ākhīrah: The Final Life or the Next Life, refers to the eternal life after death

'akhlāq: morals or etiquette. (pl. of khuluq)

'ālim: scholar

'awliyā':	*pl*. of walī
bid'ah:	innovation, usually relating to that in the religion
dīn:	way of life or religion
dirham:	a word originating from Persian, it was and is a unit of currency used in some Arab and Muslim lands. Traditionally it was made of pure silver
du'ā':	supplication
dunyā:	*lit*. translated as "closest". It refers to the current life humans live from birth to death; in opposition with the hereafter, that the human soul accesses after death
fatwā:	legal Islamic ruling
faḍā'il:	*pl*. of faḍīlah, which is an act of virtue or moral standing
fiqh:	*lit*. understanding / comprehension; and refers to the understanding of the intricates of Islamic jurisprudence
ghusl:	Ritual washing which encompasses all the body and hair
hadith:	*lit*. something new or new speech. Islamically, it refers to the narration(s) from the Prophet ﷺ or those around him. Hadith is transmitted through a chain of narration.

hajj: The pilgrimage to the House of Allah in Makkah. An annual recurrence, that an able Muslim is required to perform once in a lifetime

halal: Permitted / Allowed. Refers to what is lawful in Islam

ḥarām: Prohibited / disallowed. Refers to what is unlawful in Islam

hijrah: Migration

'ibādah: worship. In Islam. 'ibādah has a wide implication to mean any act which is done seeking the pleasure of Allah

ikhlāṣ: sincerity

'iḥsān: beautification, perfection or excellence. It is a higher form of belief about attempting the best in one's behaviour and actions. The Prophet e defined it as "worshipping Allah as if you can see Him."

imam: a leader. In Islam, it refers to a type of leadership position, most commonly used as the title of the one who leads the prayer in a mosque, or the leader of a Muslim community or people

īmān: belief

in sha Allah: if Allah wills / hopefully

isnād: chain of transmission of a narration

istinjā': act of cleansing oneself after relieving oneself

'i'tikāf:	seclusion or spiritual retreat, usually done in the masjid
Jannah:	*lit*. Garden. In the Islamic vocabulary, it refers to Paradise: the eternal Garden of the Hereafter awarded to those who have belief and are righteous. Sometimes it is translated as "Heaven" which is not strictly correct
jihād:	*lit*. striving or struggling, especially with a praiseworthy aim. In an Islamic context, it can refer to almost any effort to make personal and social life conform with Allah's guidance, such as struggle against one's evil inclinations, or one's enemies be they the devils or humans. In classical Islamic law, the term refers to armed struggle against warring disbelievers
karāmāh:	(*pl*. karāmāt) means a nobility or generous gift. It is simply translated as a miracle: which is an extraordinary and welcome event that is not explicable by natural or scientific laws and is therefore attributed to divine agency.
Laylatul Qadr:	The Night of Decree or The Night of Power
masjid:	*lit*. a place to perform prostrations, Mosque
miḥrāb:	a niche / recess in the wall of a mosque, at the point facing Makkah, towards which the congregation faces to pray
muḥaddith:	Hadith scholar or hadith narrator

mukhaḍḍram: someone who has lived through several epochs. In Islamic context refers to someone who was alive during the life of the Prophet e but never met him; and lived after him.

mursal: type of hadith transmission in which the name and person of the companion narrating from the Prophet ﷺ is missing in the chain

mustaqīm: straight

nafs: soul / self / ego

qadar: restriction or fixed portion, refers to pre-destined or pre-determined portion

qārī: a reciter of the Quran, who also memorises the whole Quran [usually]

rawḍah: (*pl*. riyāḍ) a garden or meadow, or it can refer to an interior garden or courtyard associated with the house or palace architecture

ṣaḥīḥ: *lit*. correct; in the context of hadith means authentic. If used with a capital letter it refers to the hadith books which have carried the same name, as their authors have been vigorous in choosing the narrations. The top two Sahih books are that of Imams al-Bukhārī and Muslim. The other two – which are less vigorous are that of Imams Ibn Khuzaymah and ibn Hibbān

ṣalāh:	is translated by Prayer. Its Arabic meaning is to communicate. However, it is usually used to denote a set of actions and sayings which are performed in a set way beginning with intention and ending with salutation
ṣāliḥīn:	righteous, good people
shari'a:	Islamic canonical law based on the teachings of the Quran and the *Sunnah*. It details aspects of personal and communal life from as basic as personal hygiene to as complex as governance and economics
shaykh:	refers to someone who has reached a pinnacle of something. It is therefore used for the chief of an Arab tribe, family, or village; or an old man; or someone of significant Islamic knowledge
Shaytān:	Satan. Also, means a devil. (*pl*. shayātīn)
siwāk:	Toothbrush (any type), customarily from the roots / branches of trees
Subḥān Allah:	No precise translation; but can be understood as: "Glory be to Allah" or "Allah is Perfect" or "How Free of any Imperfection is Allah" or "May He Be Exalted"
Sunnah:	*lit*. means the path or way. In Islam, it refers to the actions, words and affirmations of the Prophet Muhammad ﷺ as his mission was to show us the path to worship Allah and stay connected to Him. (*pl*. sunan)

takbīr: to say "Allahu Akbar" meaning Allah is Greater (Greatest).

taqwā: Piety / God Consciousness

tayammum: Dry ablution using earth in a specific manner

ummah: group of people, used for a small community or a large nation

walī: a difficult word to translate. It can be translated as someone who has a wonderful connection with Allah, to the extent that he loves Allah and Allah loves him. He is guided, protected and honoured by Allah. Part of Allah's honour is to bestow on him noble gifts and extraordinary occurrences knows as *karāmāt*

wūdū': ablution. In Islam, it is the set of actions which include washing and wiping set parts of the body, to make *ṣalāh* permissible to perform

zāhid: ascetic

zakah: refers to the obligatory charity that a Muslim must give, usually every year. The two main types of Zakah are Zakat ul-Fitr and Zakat ul-Mal (Zakah on the annual savings)

Translator's Biography

Leaving Iraq at a young age, Dr Omer El-Hamdoon was raised up in the UK, living in London, Bradford, Sheffield, Humberside and Kent. His role as a community leader has also taken him further afield in the UK and internationally.

His passion for understanding and teaching Islam continued to increase throughout the years, and led him to delve deep into Islamic Sciences. He is double qualified with a Masters in each of Dentistry and Islamic Studies.

For over 25 years, Shaykh Omer has been delivering Jumu'ah sermons, motivational reminders and inspiring talks; as well as regular study circles and educational courses.

As a mentor and spiritual coach, he accompanies Muslims as they work on breaking the barriers standing between them and becoming their better selves, allowing their faith to radiate in every aspect of their lives.

His traditional study of Islam compiled with his knowledge of western societies make him very aware of the gap that needs bridging for Muslims living in the West; to understand and make sense of this beautiful religion within the context of their lives. Shaykh Omer combines traditional understanding of Islam with modern concepts.

He is the co-author of the book: "30 Steps Towards a Refreshing Ramadan", where he smartly conjures up some of the deepest concepts of Islam with a cocktail of technological terms, inviting the reader to dwell into the spiritual aspects of Ramadan, by relating the jargon of modern gadgets to one's inner soul (nafs).